✳ Advance Praise for PURELY ALASKA ✳

Here are the beginnings of a true ~~~~~~~~ ern
rural Alaska. These stories descri ~~~~~~~~ -
of-fact style. Within the raw imn ~~~~~~~~ es,
we find great human themes of life in transition ~p~
redemption and exaltation—all depicted before the astonishing
backdrop of Alaska's natural and cultural landscapes.
　　　　　—**Tom Kizzia**, author of *The Wake of the Unseen Object*

These stories leap to the true side of things in our state, leaving
behind the cardboard myth of Alaska—a good thing, and a great read.
　　　　　—**Seth Kantner**, author of *Ordinary Wolves*

This is a wonderful collection—a delight to read. Professors Andrews
and Creed have done a remarkable job, not only of attending the
birth of these thirty-two tales and navigating the group into print,
but as guides who for more than twenty years have led residents of
Alaska's outback into the adventure of writing.
　　　　　—**Dan O'Neill**, author of *The Firecracker Boys*

A major contribution to Far North literature, *Purely Alaska* honors
the challenges, traditions, and wisdom of remote Alaska.
　　　　　—**Jerah Chadwick**, former Alaska Poet Laureate

Purely Alaska escorts readers on an unadulterated journey into the
heart and soul of rural Alaska. This anthology should be a top choice
for educators seeking to ignite classrooms with the spark of insight,
the fire of authenticity, the radiance of truth. *Purely Alaska* speaks
directly and honestly.
　　　　　—**Sandra Shroyer-Beaver**, president, board of
　　　　　education, and **Dr. Norman Eck**, superintendent,
　　　　　Northwest Arctic Borough School District

The storytellers' settings are unforgettable, the adventures are
remarkable, and the voices are inspirational. These are stories Alaska
can't afford to lose.
　　　　　—**Sherry Simpson**, author of *The Accidental Explorer*

PURELY ALASKA
Authentic Voices from the Far North

Stories from 23 rural Alaskans
Edited by Susan B. Andrews & John Creed

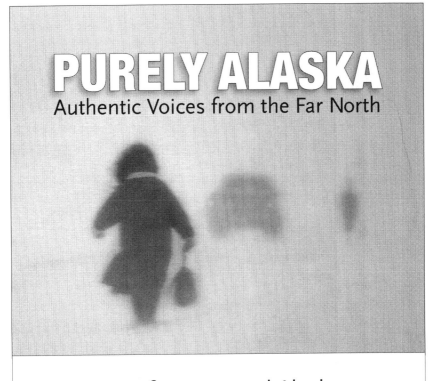

PURELY ALASKA
Authentic Voices from the Far North

Stories from 23 rural Alaskans
Edited by Susan B. Andrews & John Creed

STEVE WERLE + SUSAN B. ANDREWS + JOHN CREED + IVA BAKER + R.A. DILLON
NANCY BERKEY + MARCUS MILLER + KARL PUCKETT + BURTON W. HAVILAND JR.
AMY REISLAND-SPEER + GINA POPE + JOLI MORGAN + LUCY DANIELS + CHINA KANTNER
SONJA WHITETHORN + STEVE PILZ + EMMA SNYDER + ROBERT ANDREWS
KATHRYN LENNIGER + WILMA PAYNE + TERRY WILSON + AL BOWLING + KATIE CRUTHERS

Epicenter Press is a regional press publishing nonfiction books about the arts, history, environment, and diverse cultures and lifestyles of Alaska and the Pacific Northwest.

Publisher: Kent Sturgis
Acquisitions Editor: Lael Morgan
Editors: Susan B. Andrews & John Creed
Proofreader: Sherrill Carlson
Cover design: Leslie Newman, Newman Design/Illustration
Cover photos: (front) white-out blizzard by Al Bowling
    (back) Amy Reisland-Speer and Della Keats by John Creed;
    Susan Andrews & John Creed by Nelson's Photography, Fairbanks, Alaska
Text design & production: Leslie Newman & Katie Meyer
Printer: Thomson-Shore, Inc.

Library of Congress Control Number: 2010927450
ISBN 978-1-935347-10-1
10 9 8 7 6 5 4 3 2
Printed in the United States of America

To order single copies of this title, mail $17.95 plus $6.00 for shipping (WA residents add $2.15 state sales tax) to Epicenter Press, PO Box 82368, Kenmore, WA 98028; call us at 800-950-6663, or visit www.EpicenterPress.com. Contact the publisher regarding volume discounts.

ACKNOWLEDGMENTS

WE THANK the following individuals and groups for their assistance in the preparation of *Purely Alaska*.

Current and Former Chukchi College, University of Alaska, Staff and Faculty: Christine Erlich, Mary Booth-Barger, Byrd Norton, Donene Stein, Spring Pungowiyi, Valarie Romane, Katie Cruthers, Donna Westdahl, Susan Warner, Patricia Harding, Tom Pennington, Stacey Glaser, Greg Garrett, Maureen Nolan, John Erlich, Danija Groves, E. Robert Mackey, Jane Winzer, Karen Hadley, Minnie Naylor, Annette Richards, Ruthie Sampson, Diane Okleasik, Pauline Harvey.

Anchorage Daily News past and present editors: David Hulen, Steve Lindbeck, Larry Persily, Matt Zencey, and Frank Gerjevic; Fairbanks Daily News-Miner: Rod Boyce, managing editor; Alaska Newspapers, Inc. & The Arctic Sounder: former editors Randall Howell, Beth Ipsen & current editor, Victoria Barber; Larry Campbell, Alaska's former Associated Press bureau chief, current managing editor, Peninsula Clarion; The Anchorage Press, former editors, Robert Meyerowitz and Lynne Snifka; Dennis Zaki, AlaskaReport.com; Tony Hopfinger & Amanda Coyne, AlaskaDispatch.com; Shannyn Moore, KBYR-AM; Phil Munger, ProgressiveAlaska.blogspot.com; Dan O'Neill, Fairbanks.

Other individuals: Jude Baldwin, former museum librarian, Anchorage Museum of History and Art; Kathleen Hertel-Baker, director, Library and Archives, Anchorage Museum at Rasmuson Center; Mary Anne Slemmons, library assistant, historical collections, Alaska State Library; Sandra Johnston, library assistant, historical collections, Alaska State Library; Barry McWayne, coordinator, fine arts, University of Alaska Museum of the North; Arlene Schmuland, Archives and Manuscripts Department, University of Alaska Anchorage; Helen D. Reavis and Nicole Page of Reavis Parent Lehrer LLP, New York City; Al Bowling, Anchorage; Jim Magdanz, Kotzebue; David Duplessis, Sundog Media; Professor Emeritus Jerah Chadwick, Aleutian Pribilof Center, Interior-Aleutians Campus, UAF; Professor Ron Illingworth, Interior-Aleutians Campus, UAF; George Guthridge, Bristol Bay Campus, UAF; Carolyn Kremers, Fairbanks; Sherry Modrow & Brian Rogers, UAF Chancellor.

We are indebted to Gary Dunham, our former editor at the University of Nebraska Press, and Robert Mandel, director, Texas Tech University Press, for supporting the project through its various permutations.

Many thanks to Dan Julius, vice president, academic affairs, University of Alaska Statewide, for underwriting the voicesofalaska. com website.

We are forever inspired by former UAF Professor Rick Steiner for standing up for academic freedom.

Special thanks to our children, Myles, Tiffany, Trevor and Deirdre Creed as well as to our extended families.

A special recognition to our editor and publisher, the unflappable Kent Sturgis. Thank you, Kent, for your extraordinary editing talent, knowledge of Alaska, and deep respect for this work, including appreciating this anthology's merit from the very start.

We extend our deepest thanks to our students, past and present, for your constant inspiration.

Caribou migration

CONTENTS

* * * * * * * * * * * *

Sunlight on an autumn evening drenches
Kotzebue and the surrounding hills

Chukchi College in Kotzebue is one of six branch
campuses of the University of Alaska Fairbanks.

INTRODUCTION

In the immense, roadless expanse of the Far North, story-telling has thrived for many generations. Stories range from harrowing survival adventures to tales of other exotic people, places, and cultures. This anthology captures some of these stories as told by rural Alaskans.

Before we began teaching for the University of Alaska, we made our living in journalism, a thrilling and fascinating profession, whose core is storytelling.

In the late 1980s, we switched from writing news to the teaching of writing at Chukchi College, a branch of UA Fairbanks in Kotzebue, also called *Qikiqtagruk*, which means "almost an island" in Iñupiaq Eskimo. Kotzebue, the trade and transportation hub for ten northwest Alaska villages, sits on a narrow gravel spit that stabs the often treacherous Chukchi Sea some twenty-six miles inside the Arctic Circle and about 175 miles northeast of Russia's eastern tip.

Most of our students we never see. While some live in Kotzebue, our "classroom" stretches far from Kotzebue, to southeast Alaska, 1,000 miles away; to eastern Alaska along the Canadian border and farther into the Interior; to southwest Alaska's Bethel region; and out onto the Aleutian Islands. We reach students using satellite- and computer-assisted technology, the telephone, and the U.S. mail.

Most of our students are pursuing a degree or certificate from one of Alaska's three public universities: UA Fairbanks, UA Anchorage, or the Juneau-based UA Southeast. Most live in small, isolated communities. They range from a precocious eleven-year-old to senior citizens; most students fall outside the typical college age.

A big majority of our students are women. They are single, married with kids, perhaps hold a full-time job in the village. They share a passion to earn a degree or certificate in education, health, social work, or rural development, taking one or two courses at a time. Also enrolled are bright, motivated high school students seeking a college-preparatory challenge. Our students include many middle-aged people and elders looking to finish work toward a degree. Other students enroll to sharpen job skills or for personal interest. Whatever their reasons, our students typically live miles from the nearest road to the outside world.

Early on, we realized that our students were writing about life experiences that would intrigue an audience beyond our classroom. We figured Alaska's print media might be interested in publishing perspectives from Alaska's most remote communities. In the early days, we used a brand-new technology, the fax machine, to send a few stories to some newspaper editors. They gladly published them. Soon we decided to give this fledgling "cultural journalism" project a name: Chukchi News and Information Service.

Cultural journalism is a genre of writing and photography that neither reports "news" nor fits in with the traditional opinion writing that appears on a newspaper's editorial pages. Instead of covering out-of-the-ordinary occurrences that typically constitute news coverage, cultural journalism focuses on the more ordinary rhythms of life and voices largely missing from the traditional media.

Eventually this publication effort would expand statewide after its start in Kotzebue's weekly newspaper, *The Arctic Sounder*, and the now-defunct statewide Native weekly, *Tundra Times*. By the early 1990s, the writing project had captured several high-profile state and national awards. In the mid-1990s, Chukchi News and Information Service was a regular feature in the *Anchorage Daily News*, Alaska's largest newspaper. In 1998, the University of Nebraska Press published a best-selling volume of student stories from the project, called *Authentic Alaska: Voices of Its Native Writers*. In the ensuing years, our students' work still appears in various print publications, but reflecting the Internet age, often it appears on websites and blogs as opposed to hard copy.

This volume is a sequel to *Authentic Alaska*. The majority of writers whose work appears here have lived in rural Alaska for many years. They offer a unique voice to the mix of writing about rural Alaska. These stories come from those who know rural Alaska best: the people who live here. This anthology offers glimpses of regular people meeting life's everyday challenges while experiencing the same struggles, joys, and idiosyncrasies that humans face everywhere: adolescents coming of age, struggles with addiction, regional idioms, and cross-cultural challenges. Some stories cover experiences more specific to Alaska, such as dog-mushing and Native language. All are set in this vast chunk of remote North America called rural Alaska, where caribou, moose, and bears far outnumber the people.

Most of the work in *Purely Alaska* is being published for the first time. Some of the stories were completed as an assignment in a writing class, while others took on a life of their own as students continued to write beyond formal coursework but still collaborating with their professors. We selected stories for this volume that we believe best reflect rural Alaska.

In 1999, Richard K. Nelson of Sitka, a literary non-fiction author, became the first Alaska State Writer Laureate. Nelson, an anthropologist, lived and worked for many years in northern villages, including the northwest arctic region. Nelson urges all Alaskans to use words and images to document life in rural Alaska.

"That's where I think the growth of literature in Alaska is going to be really important—people capturing the essence of life in Alaska at this time," Nelson told the *Sitka Sentinel*.

"These writers are putting down in writing a way of life that will not exist fifty years from now," he said. "Alaska is changing rapidly, and this literature that's emerging in Alaska today is going to be a treasure for future generations of Alaskans."

We hope this book further enriches that literary legacy. We hope this anthology reveals in a real, even raw way, something genuine and honest. We hope it offers truth, coming as it does, directly and from the heart. We hope you enjoy these stories, told in unassuming voices against the backdrop of extraordinary places.

We believe these authentic voices are, indeed, purely Alaska.

Susan B. Andrews and John Creed

ARCTIC OCEAN

ALASKA

bler

Fairbanks
○
■
Nenana

Denali
National Park
and Preserve

McGrath
■

Anchorage
○

Kokhanok
■

Haines ■

GULF OF ALASKA

■ Petersburg

Thorne Bay ■

PACIFIC OCEAN

A storm blowing in from the Bering Sea
creates whiteout conditions in Kotzebue.

※

SURVIVAL

SURVIVAL IN RURAL ALASKA historically required an extensive understanding of the state's challenging physical environment including the land, the waterways, the climate, the flora, and the fauna. This is crucial for cross-country travel through the wilderness.

For example, in the first story, Steve Werle tells of an esteemed Iñupiaq elder, the late Nellie Woods, whose intimate familiarity with arctic-survival skills proved invaluable during an extraordinary journey that took her across the North Slope in the 1930s as part of a reindeer drive intended to bring a new food source to starving Inuit in northern Canada.

Then, Werle becomes the subject of a story, as Susan B. Andrews and John Creed relate a life-threatening episode in Werle's life when he took a little spin out of Noatak on his snowmachine one winter afternoon. He is slammed down by a ferocious storm after his machine breaks down, and he narrowly escapes death.

Other writers also attest to the care and skills still necessary to survive in rural Alaska. Potential injury and even death still lurk everywhere despite Alaska's technological life-saving advancements in recent decades.

Iva Baker cares for dozens of sled dogs with her husband John Baker, who for many years has been a top contender in the annual Iditarod Trail Sled Dog Race. She tells how she narrowly escaped being stomped by a moose minutes away from home on a routine training run. Likewise, journalist R.A. Dillon could have succumbed to dark December's extreme arctic temperatures while running his first middle-distance sled-dog race north from

Kotzebue to the village of Noatak and back. Nancy Berkey's story shows how Alaska's remoteness and limited access to medical assistance can age a person prematurely, while contributor Marcus Miller manages to find humor in Alaska's sometimes dangerous commercial-fishing industry.

Karl Puckett's first winter in the state in Kotzebue in the late 1980s proved to be one of Alaska's most severe in many years, humbling this proud Minnesotan who mistakenly thought his home state's winters could match harsh winters anywhere.

In the final story, we journey with Burton Haviland, Jr. into the depths of his heart and soul to witness the stark reality of one man's hard-fought battle with addiction. His is a profound tale of survival no less courageous and daunting than anyone else's story. His is a never-ending struggle to manage demons that require a deliberate, one-day-at-a-time contract with life and a conscious, pro-active decision not to "get high." Perhaps this brutally honest story will help us to understand better this powerful, destructive affliction while offering insight for those still coping with addiction in their own lives.

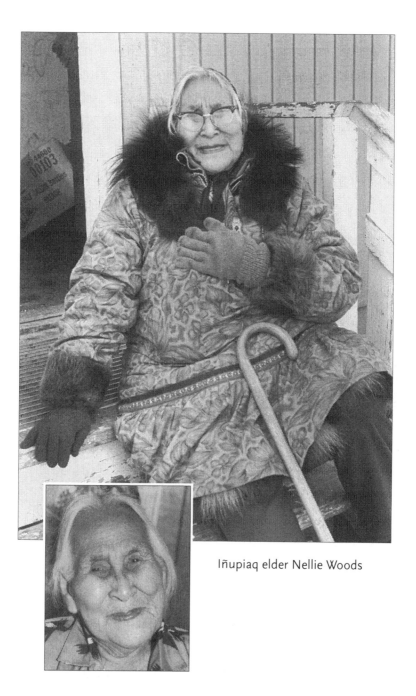

Iñupiaq elder Nellie Woods

1

* * * * * * * * * * *

~ NOATAK ~

The reindeer drive to Canada
Steve Werle

EYES FLARING WITH EMOTION, Nellie Nakauraq Woods sits on the floor in her modest home, arthritis-ravaged legs tucked beneath her faded blue-flowered *atikluk* (traditional ladies' hooded shift), its pleated flounce splayed out like a schoolgirl's skirt. A cheerful afternoon sun creates a soft halo of wispy gray hairs that have escaped from the tight bun at the back of Nellie's head. She pauses, frozen in time, *uluaq* (a traditional woman's knife, also known as a ulu knife) poised above a small plate of boiled seal meat. Steam and the soft scent of seal oil waft up from her interrupted lunch. She glances down at the torn black and white photograph of a beautiful young woman and a little girl standing side by side in their best parkas, this old woman and her oldest daughter, a lifetime ago.

Perched on Nellie's window sill, a portable radio crackles out *Tundra Telegraph* on KOTZ-AM, touting itself as "the only station serving northwest Alaska and eastern Siberia." In this roadless region the size of Indiana, accessible primarily by aircraft, KOTZ radio provides an important link between families and friends in far-flung camps. Folks throughout the region, populated primarily by Iñupiaq Eskimos, send frequent messages over its airwaves. Nellie likes to listen for familiar names. Overhead, a single-engine Cessna bush plane roars toward the airport in Nellie's hometown of Noatak, laden with another load of mail and groceries. Snowmobiles and four-wheelers buzz up and down the snow-covered gravel street just outside Nellie's frame house, a home so starkly different from the tiny one-room log houses and canvas tents that sheltered her youth. Indeed, life has changed much from when Nellie Woods' young legs carried her for endless miles across Alaska's northern tundra.

Aana (grandmother) Nellie, as this esteemed elder is known by virtually everyone in her world, gazes unseeing into the distance, the past washing over her, eyes moistened with pain. She has been asked to dredge up memories of a two-year trek made decades before—memories that encompass the difficulty of birth, a harsh everyday life, and the almost unbearably painful death of a loved one. The journey's hardships, buried beneath two generations of busy family life, cascade across half a century and intrude into the present.

"So long ago," she murmurs, mostly to herself, "So long ago."

August 17, 1931. A young, vibrant, twenty-three-year-old Nellie Woods has floated down the Noatak River from her inland home. She stands on Front Street in the tiny coastal village of Kotzebue, twenty-six miles above the Arctic Circle in northwest Alaska. A chilly breeze off the ocean ruffles the wolverine fur framing her face, which is seasoned a deep brown after a summer of busy subsistence routine under the perpetual arctic sun. Obsidian eyes gaze across the flat brown water of Kotzebue Sound, where a tiny dot on the horizon indicates a fifteen-ton schooner called the *Hazel*. In the expanse of the arctic, this ship resembles but a mere dust mote. But for the next month, Nellie and a handful of other passengers will call this unfamiliar vessel home as it carries them ever farther from their beloved homeland.

The comforting weight of Nellie's infant daughter wiggles against her back beneath her parka as her gaze shifts toward the north, where heat waves from the high arctic sun quaver and dance, blending sky, land, and water into a shimmering collage. Although too far to see with her eyes, Nellie's mind easily focuses on her family camp at Sealing Point, forty miles farther up the coast, her birthplace twenty-three years ago to the day, in 1908. A smile flickers across her face as she remembers the black sand beaches that provided driftwood, shells, and other treasures for her happy childhood. Nellie can almost hear the few rusty fox traps that would be rattling against a tent frame in the continuous ocean breeze. The tent frame and drying racks, made of spruce poles carried from the Noatak valley, would be standing like skeletons against the bisected horizon of black water to the west and undulating golden tundra toward the east. In her mind, Nellie can smell the mild seal-oil scent as she pictures her mother hunched over the skin of a bearded seal, her *ulu* flashing in the sun as she cuts long strips of black meat to dry. Another rack would have golden rows of trout, sliced in perfect horizontal strips, glowing like edible artwork in the sun. Later, as an adult, these memories of summer camp would flood Nellie Nakauraq Woods with the warm comfort and satisfaction of a bountiful land and a satisfying life.

Nellie never questions the need to go far away from this home she loves. Her husband needs her and she will suffer any doubt, suffer any fear, in silence. She does what needs to be done, and she undoubtedly will call on all her Sealing Point subsistence skills to stay alive on this reindeer-herding journey.

On her twenty-third birthday, Nellie forsakes the familiar comfort of her homeland for the rough wooden decks of a stranger's ship.

Weeks before, Nellie had received a message to join her husband, Peter, on the North Slope, the flat coastal plane that marks the northernmost boundary of Alaska and the beginning of the Arctic Ocean. A year earlier, Peter, a hardworking and experienced reindeer herder, had joined the effort to drive a 3,000-head reindeer herd from the Seward Peninsula south of Kotzebue all the way to the Mackenzie River in Canada's Northwest Territories. On a map, the route spans more than 1,000 miles, but the daunting reality of the trek would prove much more in hardship. The early part of the route crossed the Brooks Range through an area that even the Indigenous people

Nellie never questions the need to go far away from this home she loved. Her husband needed her and she would suffer any doubt, suffer any fear, in silence.

avoided in the winter, where wind and cold could be so brutal that even the superbly adapted caribou sometimes froze to death. Yet a dozen men, with little support or outside contact, faced this forbidding territory. As if the trip alone were not difficult enough, the tiny band was charged with coercing thousands of semi-domesticated animals, whose primary instinct was to return to familiar range, to go with them.

A dozen men had begun the trip near the present-day village of Deering with 3,450 reindeer, moving their gear on fourteen sleds pulled by sixteen trained reindeer. During the first winter, the herd moved less than 200 miles. Surrendering to frostbite, sickness, or exhaustion, several members of the party had to quit within a few months. At the junction of the Hunt and Kobuk rivers, still south of the Brooks Range, the drive halted for the summer of 1930 while experienced Iñupiaq reindeer herders, including Peter Woods, were recruited to join the drive.

Peter Woods numbered among the many Iñupiat who embraced reindeer-herding in a successful transition from a pure subsistence way of life to a more cash-based, western economy. Peter Woods had begun his reindeer career in 1907 with Kotzebue's "mission herd." Early reindeer herds were owned by the Friends Church, and Native herders contracted to tend the animals in payment for a few deer each year. Nellie also had grown up following reindeer with her family. Nellie's father, George Sheldon, had been a successful herder in the Noatak region for many years, and Nellie and her family often traveled with the herds.

In 1889, the first reindeer had been imported to northwestern Alaska from Siberia by the historically controversial Sheldon Jackson, a Presbyterian minister and General Agent for Education for the territory of Alaska. In addition to helping create a reliable food source for local Natives, Jackson also sought to "civilize" the Eskimos and to "educate" them in western ways, but most of all he was promoting a new religion called Christianity.

Building on his initial success with Siberian reindeer, Jackson bought additional deer from Lapp herders in Norway. These reindeer eventually created the core of an industry that helped sustain Iñupiaq Eskimos of northwest Alaska during a low cycle in game populations during the late 1800s, known in Alaska history as "the great famine." Caribou populations crashed drastically at a time when whale, walrus, and other marine mammals had been decimated by Yankee whalers from New England. To add to the food scarcity, even salmon runs dipped into a low cycle during these years. The food crisis, in conjunction with diseases brought by outside contact, decimated entire villages.

Jackson's reindeer multiplied rapidly, grazing on the lush tundra formerly utilized by the caribou, and by 1930, nearly every Native village between Nome and Barrow was involved in reindeer herding. The Canadian government, in an effort to duplicate Alaska's success, contracted with the Lomen Company to drive Alaska brood stock into Canada for Eskimos in the northern Yukon and Northwest Territories. Managed by brothers Carl, Alfred, and Ralph Lomen, the Lomen Company operated the largest reindeer operation in the territory. Peter Woods had managed Lomen herds for many years, in addition to developing his own smaller herd. When the drive to Canada faltered, the Lomen brothers called on trustworthy and skilled herders such as Peter Woods to complete the monumental task.

Although the drive officially began the day after Christmas in 1929, preparations had been years in the making. In an attempt to determine the feasibility of the trip, the Canadian government had hired Danish explorer Erling Porsild to survey possible routes. During 1927 and 1928, Porsild traveled by canoe, dog team, and on foot from Nome in western Alaska to Aklavik, an Inuit settlement on the Mackenzie River delta in Canada's Northwest Territories. Porsild focused on two main routes: follow the arctic coast around the perimeter of Alaska, or trudge northeast and inland through tenuous passes in the formidable Brooks Range. Porsild suggested the coastal route for many reasons: it contained better grazing for reindeer; the terrain was much less rugged; and the coastal route would enjoy numerous human settlements that could supply and support the herders. The Lomen brothers, however, rejected the coastal route for the same reasons that made it the better choice. The numerous Native villages along this route had their own reindeer herds, and the Lomens feared their stock would join the Native herds. But the preferred inland route would take its toll on the men and reindeer alike.

While Peter, the reindeer, and his fellow herders were struggling toward their distant Canadian destination, back in Noatak his young bride, Nellie, enjoyed none of today's modern luxuries of phone calls, letters, or messages on the radio from her husband during the year they were separated. At best, Nellie relied on sporadic relays from bush pilots who had dropped off supplies and monitored the herd's progress. When Nellie finally got word to join the drive, the herders had managed to push 3,000 obstinate reindeer over the Brooks Range, across a vast treeless plain, and onto the shore of the ice-choked Beaufort Sea far to the north. But the men were exhausted, their skin clothing in tatters, their spirit spent. They needed the reinforcement of fresh manpower and boy power as well as hard-working wives like Nellie before another brutal northern winter descended upon them again.

Despite her youth, Nellie was no stranger to travel. Indeed, she had spent her entire life flowing with the natural rhythms of her people's traditionally nomadic way of life. The arctic wilderness landscape, within a 200-mile radius of Noatak, comprised her ancestral homeland. She knew the place-name of every mountaintop or river bend, not as a feature on some map, but as a landmark related to the Iñupiaq way of life. Each place was named after an important event or a visible feature. A map would call a river the Kelly, named after an early white explorer, but Nellie knew it better as the *Kuugruuraq*, or little river, where she could catch large trout most of the year.

Since before she could remember, like untold generations before her, Nellie began every spring with an annual migration from the protectively wooded, inland Noatak River valley, where her family spent the winter subsisting on the bounty of fall's harvest, to the windswept, treeless coast of the Chukchi Sea. Spring was the time for hunting *ugruk* (bearded seals) for their tasty meat in addition to that staple of every traditional Iñupiaq meal, seal oil. Belugas were harvested for their white *muktuk* (whale skin with blubber). Arctic char, salmon, ducks, eggs, and, later, beach greens, and berries kept every family member busy gathering the

Reindeer herding, circa 1913-39, Alaska Peninsula

natural bounty of this challenging land. By August, heavily loaded boats pulled along the shore by dogs and people, or, in favorable winds, pushed along by sails, would begin the journey up the Noatak River alongside the soon-to-be-spawning salmon. Later, the men would hunt caribou when their migration route crossed the river. Then, the family would settle into its winter camp for another season in the mountain-framed Noatak valley.

Yet, the trip that began in the summer of 1931 would be different. Nellie would not be traveling with her family and their possessions in their skin boat, searching for the wild foods that had sustained her people for centuries. This time, she and a handful of other women and children were putting their trust in a stranger, Captain August Masik. This boisterous, blue-eyed giant of a *naluagmiu* (the Iñupiaq name for white man, meaning "inhabitant of bleached seal skin") with unusually light hair looked and acted so different from the local people that he intimidated his quiet passengers. He aptly fit his Eskimo name, *Kasaluk*, which means "big fellow." As a trader who had plied these extreme northern waters for years, and who was known as an honest man, Captain Masik was paid $500 by the Lomen Company to haul

Nellie and other family members to the North Slope along with his regular trade goods.

More than once, tossing about aboard ship, Nellie longed for the soft support of familiar tundra beneath her feet, and feared for her and her child's safety as fall storms buffeted the ship like an insignificant piece of driftwood. Day and night, the steam-powered vessel relentlessly churned its way up the coast.

As the ship rounded Point Barrow on the eastward leg of its journey, a cold wind screamed off the arctic ice pack. Despite the wind, though, the offshore ice reduced the waves and made for smoother sailing. Finally, Nellie and the other passengers could safely move around on deck and survey their new surroundings. Nellie's concern over the impending winter deepened with the thickening layer of ice on their water supply. Snow already was creeping down the far-off hills as they anchored off Foggy Island, just east of present-day Prudhoe Bay, in late September.

Nellie and Peter's happy reunion barely moved beyond a warm embrace before everyone began working feverishly to prepare for the coming winter and the drive's expected culmination in the spring. Unbeknownst to the herders, however, the most difficult phase of the drive still was ahead, and they would face three more grueling winters, and still not reach the drive's terminus.

"*Aarigaa*," Aana Nellie sighs and shakes her head. She utters this all-purpose Iñupiaq expression for wistful emphasis to convey her recollection of so long ago when she was an eager young woman bearing scant knowledge of what the near future would hold for her and her family.

Humans and reindeer alike had been worn thin by the drive. The herd had been at rest for many weeks, waiting for the tundra's summer sponge to freeze solid enough for more efficient travel.

When the trek resumed in late October, trained reindeer pulled sleds loaded with food and equipment while herders walked. When the snow deepened, herders donned skis, with one member advancing ahead of the herd to search for the next suitable campsite. Camp selection was based as much on available grazing for the deer as on the comfort of the people.

Herding reindeer does not entail a mere matter of steady

forward progress. Reindeer hate to travel with the wind because they cannot smell potential predators. In addition, being creatures of habit, they often attempt to return to their previous grazing area. Drivers must work constantly to keep them moving in the desired direction. Reindeer have little regard for the timetables of humans. To complicate matters, passing caribou herds tend to assimilate any reindeer allowed to stray from the domesticated herd. The herding instinct is strong, and reindeer will gladly join a larger group, or one that is going the direction they want to go. Often the herders are forced to backtrack with half the herd to attract dispersed reindeer, and a week's progress can be nullified by a single stampede or storm.

As the expedition continued east, winter raged across the treeless expanse of the North Slope. The herd painstakingly trudged, against its will, through the bitter winter darkness. In this land where the sun refuses to shine for almost three months, even the full moon offered more light than the weak winter daylight, glowing briefly each day from a sun lurking just below the horizon. As they walked, everyone kept close watch for driftwood, willow twigs, and even outcrops of coal. In camp, as the herders huddled in their single-wall canvas tents, the burnable materials would provide precious heat to dry sweat-soaked clothing and cook the day's food. The eight people in Nellie's tent, wearing constantly wet clothing, combined with temperatures dipping past 40 degrees below zero, created a dense ice fog in the tent. Nellie could not even see a lighted candle a few feet away.

Storms often forced the group to remain camped, but the reindeer and their herders never stopped moving about. The reindeer needed constant tending from predators and from the deer's own instincts to backtrack. Herders frequently spend more than twenty-four hours away from camp, often carrying only a blanket and a stiff piece of canvas for protection.

"Them young men never rest," Aana Nellie remembers across the decades, "always traveling."

As she shares her sympathy for the men's duties, Nellie glosses over her own grueling daily chores, pursued diligently despite the fact that she is pregnant and taking care of her young daughter

while cooking and sewing for at least eight people. Storms regularly halted the drive, and they afforded cover for the innumerable
wolves to swoop surreptitiously in and kill reindeer at every opportunity. The herders seldom ate as well as the wolves.

"We never eat the reindeer," said Aana Nellie.

Despite the thin soup that was often their only hot meal
of the day, reindeer meat on this drive was not an option, not
because the herders wouldn't relish the fresh meat, but because
the deer were the foundation that would bring prosperity to their
Inuit brothers and sisters in Canada. Besides, the deer did not
belong to the herders. They were responsible for the well-being
of the herd, and they took that duty seriously. So, in addition to
the perpetual search for fuel, every member kept a constant vigil
for food. They depended on ptarmigan, rabbits, and caribou to
supplement their stores. They sometimes caught white fox. (Aana
Nellie remembers she caught two.) Each fox skin could be traded
for $25 worth of tea, coffee, flour, and lard from the few scattered
trading posts along the coast. In this country in the 1930s, furs
were still more common currency than paper money.

Many times, though, the herders, like the reindeer, dug
beneath the snow for meager greens to supplement their diet.
Nellie accepted the lean rations, but she missed eating fish, a
mainstay in her daily diet since childhood. Her mouth watered
thinking of golden salmon, fat Noatak trout, and huge, delicious,
white-fleshed Kotzebue sheefish.

Winter retreats grudgingly on the North Slope, but eventually the ground became so soft the herders' sleds were abandoned.
Then the equipment was carried by pack deer, and by the people themselves. By the spring of 1932, Nellie was eight months
pregnant, and the journey, with its daily chores and constant
movement, continued unabated. Warm weather opened swift
rivers, another daunting obstacle. But rivers also provided Nellie's
beloved fish. Even decades later in old age, Nellie licks her lips as
she recalls the tasty meals.

"Very good," Aana Nellie says, relishing the memory. "Sweet
meat."

To ferry people and supplies across the numerous streams,

the men fashioned a boat frame out of willow sticks, while the women sewed a waterproof cover from five moose skins. After each crossing, the craft is painstakingly taken apart and loaded onto a pack deer, only to be reassembled, all too soon, for the next river crossing.

In the spring of 1932, Nellie's family left the drive and camped on the coast near the Canning River to await the birth of her child. Finally, Nellie didn't have to pack up and move daily. She could endure the last few weeks of her pregnancy in a stationary camp. In addition, a small trading post a few miles away provided the luxury of imported foods. On June 13, 1932, Nellie gave birth to a daughter, whose parents named her Helen. The family soon rejoined the drive, but progress was painfully slow until freeze-up offered solid footing once again. By winter, though, baby Helen had contracted a fever, and her health steadily declined. Now, along with the reindeer's soft grunting and the click of their hooves came the stuttering wail of the newborn. Trudging through the constant winter darkness, there was no refuge from the perpetual effort that sapped even the strongest adults. With the nearest medical assistance hundreds of miles away, Nellie was forced to depend on the few herbal remedies that she could scrounge from beneath the drifting snow. Despite all the best and sometimes frantic efforts under the circumstances, on a dark and bitterly cold December day in 1932, their precious little girl died. Grief stricken, barely able to stand, tears streaming down their cheeks, Nellie and Peter Woods set out to bury their child beneath the snow at Long Point. Squinting against the blowing snow, and her own intense pain, Nellie stared around the dark treeless landscape. No comfort could be found in the featureless dull white that blends sky, land, and water into a singular, blurry image, like the dark days and nights of this arduous trek. A soft moan escaped her lips as Nellie gazed at the tiny form bundled in a decorated caribou-skin bunting. How could she leave her baby so far from home and family? How could she go on?

Although nearly sixty winters have passed, Aana Nellie's voice cracks as the tragic memory overwhelms her.

"My baby still up there," she whispers, wiping a tear from

her eye with a trembling hand.

Despite hardship and tragic loss, Nellie never considered abandoning her duty. She continued the journey because her family counted on her support. Throughout the brutal winter of 1932 and into the spring of 1933 and then yet another slogging summer, the drive inched toward its destination. There is good reason why the wild caribou abandon these soggy plains shortly after the spring calving season. At this time of year, mosquitoes and flies constantly plague humans and reindeer alike. Reindeer lose weight from the blood loss and sometimes go mad from the vicious hordes, charging blindly across the tundra. Only constant vigilance and quick action by the herders can prevent stampedes from scattering the herd. Herders face the same droning clouds of bloodthirsty insects as the reindeer; sometimes the bugs are so thick it is difficult to breathe without inhaling mosquitoes. Often, herders resort to waving leafy branches in front of their faces to keep the marauding hordes airborne.

As spring approached, Nellie was once again with child, but during this pregnancy, she contracted a unrelenting fever. Still carrying the burden of her lost child, weakened by poor nutrition and sickness, Nellie maintained her daily work schedule without complaint. Five herders depended upon her sewing skills, and the drive must continue. Even though the summer weather is warmer, the soggy tundra is harder on mukluks than in winter. Feet and legs are immersed constantly in ice-cold water, and with each arduous step reaching high enough to clear the tundra's tall tussocks, muscles burn with an effort similar to wading through knee-deep mud. Mukluks, made from the tough lower leg skin of caribou, require constant mending and replacement. Through her grief and infirmity, however, Nellie maintained her cooking and sewing duties.

By late summer 1933, the drive had reached Herschel Island, where a Canadian contingent took over. Herschel Island boasted several trading posts and a deep-water port with dozens of boats lying at anchor. Traders from as far as 1,000 miles to the east come to Herschel Island to swap furs for supplies. Herschel Island is where Nellie and her family planned to catch a boat back home.

Nellie Woods, far left, takes part in a Christmas program in Noatak in 1979.

Although they receive a small stipend, Peter will not collect his $75 per month wages for his three years of service until after they return to Kotzebue.

Although the reindeer drive was only 200 miles from its end when Nellie left for home, it required another full year and a half to complete. But history shows that the drive was successful. Not only did the reindeer ward off imminent starvation, but they also provided the basis for a thriving Canadian reindeer industry. Even today, the offspring of those first reindeer continue to graze on Canada's northern tundra. Even though reindeer herding has declined across the top of North America, to this day herding still provides stable income for many Native families.

By September 1933, trading vessels were preparing to abandon the arctic seas before the approaching winter. Nellie's family booked passage on a three-mast schooner, the *Patterson*, for the trip home. Unfortunately, Nellie's health declined rapidly. To complicate matters, she went into labor a few days after departure and was at risk of losing her life, as well as her baby's. To improve her comfort, the captain anchored offshore from a small village. Nellie struggled to get off the ship to have her baby, for even a tent would be preferable to the cramped, constantly moving boat. But the captain, fearing for Nellie's survival, adamantly refused. Luckily, the captain's wife was an experienced nurse, and she fashioned a makeshift delivery room on board. After intense labor with Nellie drifting in and out of consciousness, she gave birth to a healthy baby girl, Maria. But the exhausted mother still fought a raging fever. When the ship reached Point Barrow, the Woods family disembarked, and Nellie was rushed to the local hospital for long-term care. Nellie took nearly a year in Barrow to recover from her ordeal, but at least she found herself among family and close friends.

When Nellie finally gained enough strength to go home, she experienced her first airplane ride. Aana Nellie smiles when she recalls her fear of that great silver, roaring, radial-engine aircraft. She thought flying in an airplane would be like riding in a dog sled, so she bundled her daughters in their warmest parkas. Nellie was amazed when she reached her destination in only a few hours. Her journey to Barrow on the boat had taken more than a month. Finally, she returned home. She held her daughters close, heart overflowing with warmth and peace, as she gazed at familiar landmarks.

Of course, Nellie's adventures did not end with the culmination of the reindeer drive. Through the ensuing years, Nellie and Peter continued their subsistence way of life in the Kotzebue region. In addition, they participated in numerous ventures, including gold-mining and hauling freight to river dwellers in their own boat, the *Helen*, named after their lost baby. Over the years, Nellie would lose two more children, sons, who lie buried on the banks of the Noatak River. She would raise several other children, natural and adopted, and touch untold lives with her humility, humor, and wit.

This smiling old woman shrugs off her life's adventures with a wave of her hand. Aana Nellie's eyes glitter like polished hematite as she laughs at the tattered photo of her youth; that young woman of so long ago shimmering just beneath the surface of her age-lined face.

"I'm just a Noatak girl," she says with a hearty laugh.

Afterword

Nellie Woods' life spanned one of the most dramatic transitions humanity has yet witnessed, from a time when most communication was limited to the oral tradition and transportation was human-powered, to satellite telephones and men walking on the moon.

Despite the astounding advances in technology she witnessed, Nellie remained firmly connected to the land. Although Nellie Woods died peacefully in her home in 1991 at the age of eighty-three, her connection to the land remains through her offspring. Many of her children, grandchildren, and great grandchildren still live in Noatak and practice subsistence activities like untold generations before, renewing their connections to this bountiful land.

Aana Nellie would be proud.

STEPHEN J. WERLE, born in 1947, has eight children—five boys and three girls. Although he grew up in Iowa, which he refers to as the land of "corn and hogs," he lived a subsistence lifestyle upon moving to Noatak in northwest Alaska in 1988. He has been a railroader, mechanic, and elementary schoolteacher. He is married to Deborah Werle, a former teacher in Noatak. He earned his bachelor of arts degree in education "almost entirely via distance education through the University of Alaska." Until he came to Alaska, he says, "I used to think I was born one-hundred years too late, but I was just a few thousand miles too far south." In 2009, he and his family returned to Minnesota to care for an ailing relative.

Outside Noatak

2

The day Steve's snowmachine broke
Susan B. Andrews and John Creed

WHAT DO YOU CALL IT? Steve Werle calls it "gettin' the stink blowed off." It is his way of dealing with the inevitable rut of everyday living that can grind us down, wherever we might live, whatever we might do, unless we regularly pursue those wonderful things in life that we truly love.

For Steve Werle, this meant venturing into the wild lands surrounding Noatak, a tightly knit Iñupiaq Eskimo village that clings to the ever-eroding banks of the Noatak River some eighty miles above the Arctic Circle in northwest Alaska.

Like many Alaskans, Steve regularly pursues his passion— subsistence hunting and fishing amid Alaska's untamed natural grandeur—by getting out of town and into the country by boat, four-wheeler, or snowmachine, depending on the season.

On a Friday afternoon in February some years ago, Steve, a trim, buoyant, middle-aged man with perpetually jovial eyes and a quick belly laugh, fired up his snowmachine and headed out of town to cure, if temporarily, that predictable buildup of everyday blues. Steve wasn't planning to hunt or fish. He wanted to photograph the wreckage of a mail plane that had crashed a couple of days earlier on a mountaintop out toward the coast. He thought he might offer a photo and a story to the region's weekly paper, *The Arctic Sounder*.

This "mere afternoon jaunt," as Steve recalled it, would take a few hours. He would be home for supper.

Steve cruised west through the craggy black spruce and low, dense willows that hug the Noatak River basin but soon give way to the bald and rounded Mulgrave Hills that, on a clear day, offer unobstructed views in all directions. To the south, the ever-widening Noatak River delta spreads shallow and wide until it braids into the gleaming expanse of Kotzebue Sound.

At times, Steve felt as if he were floating above the brilliant white snow and mysterious winter light splaying across February's long-shadowed landscape. He inhaled the crisp, clean air. The fiery red ball of a low-lying winter sun shimmered in the southern sky.

As Steve neared the mouth of Rabbit Creek, about twenty miles from Noatak, he was enveloped in weather that suddenly became ugly. Winds began thrashing out of the west off the frozen Chukchi Sea and slamming into the treeless distant coast over the hills. Serious mischief was ushering itself into Steve's shrinking world.

Winds thrashed out of the west off the frozen Chukchi Sea and slammed into the treeless distant coast over the hills. Serious mischief was ushering itself into Steve's shrinking world.

As he looked around, sensing trouble ahead, Steve's warm home in Noatak bubbled up to the edge of his mind. Home was the preferred venue at the moment. That's where he decided to go—-and fast. Visibility plummeted to zero.

I'd better beat this bad boy back home, Steve thought, finally recognizing that he was fighting a major storm, not your average fleeting ground blizzard. Steve assumed he easily could escape to safety, as he'd done countless times before, if he kept that right thumb firmly working the throttle and traveled in the right direction.

No problem.

"I should be fine," Steve said out loud to reassure himself as he bounced across the high, rough, rolling tundra. No problem. But then, Steve's snowmachine plunged into a deep, nasty rut.

BANG!

The sudden dip in the trail thrust Steve forward. Luckily, he'd been gripping the handlebars tightly enough to hang on even as his whole body flew violently forward into the windshield. With the snowmachine tipped into the rut, Steve dismounted to inspect for damage.

Damn! He'd mangled one of his skis.

The snowmachine's left ski was twisted, virtually useless. No longer would it serve as that practical piece of elegantly contoured steel that glides passengers with little effort across the white, frozen earth. What do you do in the middle of a blistering blizzard when your snowmachine needs two skis but you've only got one? You squint your eyes, grit your teeth, and vow to plow ahead until you can go no more. Where's the choice? Steve unbolted his shattered ski, fired up his iron chariot, and pressed on toward home.

Now, Steve had to tilt his machine to the right to favor his lone remaining ski. The ungainly balancing act slowed his progress to a crawl as visibility worsened. Then, as Steve eased himself across a hardened snow berm, his snowmachine slowly toppled over and pushed him deep into the snow.

And the engine quit.

By then, winds were gusting up to fifty miles per hour. The snow roared at Steve in horizontal horror like painful little darts jabbing at every piece of exposed skin.

For years, Steve had run his own automotive-repair business in the Lower 48 states. Experienced mechanics know about every little handyman's trick to coax an internal combustion engine back to life in almost any weather. Everyone wants a guy like that as a traveling companion in remote Alaska.

On this fateful day, however, nothing worked.

All Steve could muster for his efforts to get moving again was to burn up an hour of light and his own now-precious energy. He realized that working himself to exhaustion by repeatedly pulling the starter rope would lead to sweat-induced hypothermia.

He was left with one shot at survival. He would wait out the storm in hopes it wouldn't last long. A seasoned outdoorsman, Steve burrowed himself next to his machine behind a windbreak dug up with the broken ski. Steve pulled a small tarp up over himself and tunneled in, trying to arrange as much comfort, all things considered, as his newly carved little shelf on the tundra would allow.

It wasn't much relief at all.

If only he'd been lucky enough, he thought, to break down under the sheltering canopy of a grove of benevolent spruce trees down by the river where he could survive for days protected from these fierce, relentless winds. But barren tundra offers no niche in which to hide from extreme weather. Steve could only hunker down and wait out the storm.

Meanwhile, back in the village, Steve's wife, Deborah, recognizing that her husband was overdue in dramatically changed weather conditions, knew instinctively that he was in grave danger. The day's lingering twilight gradually dwindled. The arctic's deep winter night was about to descend. The blizzard was rocking Noatak. Deborah alerted those who could help.

A search-and-rescue team of volunteers soon motored out of the village, heading directly into the deep darkness, into the brunt of the storm. Local folks know their ancestral homeland well enough to respect its history of swallowing even the most experienced, cautious traveler.

In Alaska, when someone is lost or needing help in the backcountry, dedicated men and women commit routine, selfless acts of bravery to rescue people in trouble. That often means facing conditions that threatens their own lives.

On this day, the air temperature hovered at about 10 degrees below zero Fahrenheit, within the comfortable zone for safe cross-country travel. But mix that temperature with gale-force winds, and the chill factor plunges to the equivalent of 60 to 70 degrees below zero.

The nasty storm that pinned Steve Werle down on the tundra howled all Friday night, all day Saturday, and dragged into Saturday night as darkness descended again. Knowing searchers would be looking for him, Steve concentrated on staying calm. Trying to keep warm and level-headed, he huddled hour after tedious hour against the cold, lifeless metal of his dead snowmachine. His conscience wrestled with the reality that others were risking their lives looking for him. Getting up every two or three hours to relieve himself, he struggled each time to chop away the wind-packed, cement-hard snow that had drifted over him.

On Sunday, the new day broke clear and calm. The storm had passed.

Yet, Steve remained stranded—a parched, hungry, deliriously glassy-eyed lost soul weak after two fitful, nearly sleepless nights. After so many hours of paralyzing immobility, Steve had to start moving again. He left his useless snowmachine behind and began hobbling across the tundra toward the river. His feet had become two numb, frozen stumps. He took one slow, painful step after another on a ten-mile trudge. Toward the end of the day, a single-engine search plane carrying state troopers buzzed overhead.

The glorious sight of that little bush plane triggered a guttural scream from Steve as he waved both arms frantically.

"Here I am, over here!" he shrieked. The plane's occupants did not see Steve.

The troopers did, however, spot the sun's reflection off the snowmachine a few miles away from where Steve stood wondering how much longer his numb feet would keep him upright and moving forward. He fought the seductive urge to sit down and rest, or, the horror, to lie down and go to sleep. He knew if he collapsed onto the snow, even for just a short rest, the "nirvana" stage of hypothermia might carry him into a deceptively pleasant state of bliss and almost certain death. Steve had enough of his wits left to want none of that.

He soldiered on, hours of heaving forward one painful step after the other. Thoughts of his wife and young son at home, his grown children, and his grandchildren drove him to press on. Right. Left. Right. Left. Right. Left.

Just as the trees along the Noatak River began to appear in the distance, he heard the faint hum of snowmachines. Would they find him or would the noise fade off in another direction? Just as Steve started descending back into despair, two village rescuers, Harold Mitchell and Vernon Adams, emerged on their snowmachines from the trees near the river. Luckily, they spotted Steve.

The two rescuers furnished the exhausted, thirsty, hungry man with a sandwich, hot coffee, and a ride home. News of the rescue was broadcast over KOTZ, the region's lone radio station.

In Noatak, medical professionals began circulating blood as quickly as possible back into Steve's frostbitten feet. Steve was evacuated to the regional hospital in Kotzebue. He would endure miserable weeks ahead recovering from an ordeal that someday would make for a fascinating story with grandchildren on his knee.

The frostbite treatment was successful. Steve would suffer none of the dreaded amputations that so many others had undergone in similar circumstances.

For their part, friends and family were overjoyed. But the euphoria didn't last long. Soon they would indulge in playful ribbing. Steve had no choice but to endure it good-naturedly before the incident finally faded from the collective local memory.

Without doubt Steve's body, mind, and spirit were shaken from his brush with death. But this lucky man had survived to hunt and fish again, to savor the love and security of family and community, to finish his teaching degree, to teach kindergarteners and first-graders in the Noatak school, to become the father of a baby girl, and to travel to Australia "just because I always wanted to go there and see it myself."

SUSAN B. ANDREWS lives north of the Arctic Circle in Kotzebue, Alaska, with her husband, John Creed, and family. Susan is professor of journalism and humanities at the Kotzebue branch of the University of Alaska, Chukchi College, where she has taught since 1989. Before coming to Kotzebue, she was anchor and news director at the KTVF-TV, the CBS affiliate in Fairbanks.

JOHN CREED is also professor of journalism and humanities at the University of Alaska's Chukchi College in Kotzebue, where he has distance taught site-bound students throughout Alaska since 1987. Before joining the UA faculty, he covered business and education for the *Fairbanks Daily News-Miner*.

John and Iva Baker with a treasured sled dog, Marley.

3

* * * * * * * * * * *

~ KOTZEBUE ~

Danger along the sled-dog trail
Iva Baker

IT IS A BEAUTIFUL SUNDAY MORNING, September 13, 1998. With the sun shining and the birds chirping on this cloudless day, my then-fiancé, John, his son Alex, niece Ashley, and I are at our dog-mushing and subsistence camp, *Sivulliqsi*, which means "leaders" in Iñupiaq. At the time, when we leased the camp from the Selawik Indian Reorganization Act (IRA) Council, five houses had been built. Members of the Seventh Day Adventist Church, who once were developing a potato farm called "Spud" on this site, occupied those houses in the late 1980s and early 1990s.

On this glorious fall day, John and I awoke and went to the main house to prepare breakfast. We decided on savory French toast and crispy bacon, never thinking that danger awaited our family this day. Just in time for breakfast, Alex and Ashley came into the house to wash up and eat. Soon we would hitch up the dogs and take them for a training run.

I like to read my Bible before I do anything else, but this day I said to myself, "I'll read my Bible when we take a short break." We head out the door, walking down to the dog yard. The dogs begin to bark; they know when it is time to run, and they love to howl about their imminent pleasure. Ashley and Alex help to water and harness the dogs. I decide I am going to run all three teams of eleven.

I enjoy traveling on the trail with the first team. I pass through trees and willows and feel the cool air brush through my face and hair. Staying in rhythm, the dogs are panting and pulling through thick, dark mud as no snow had yet stuck to the ground, even this late in the year. In such conditions, instead of using a dog sled, we use an unmotorized four-wheeler to train our dogs for the Iditarod Trail Sled Dog Race.

With the first team, we travel around a three-mile trail, and then head back to camp. We put an experienced leader, Blacky, with an inexperienced leader, Gopher, at the head of the second team for this training run. The dogs have enough power to drag the four-wheeler with its parking brake on. To keep them anchored, we connect a heavy-duty chain from the pickup truck to the four-wheeler. John disconnects the chain. I shout to the dogs, "Get ready! Go ahead!" and they charge ahead full strength. John fades into the distance as I head down the trail with the dogs trotting away.

The team and I are traveling steadily up and over a hill, swaying to the left and right over the zigzagging trail. We pass a moose cow and calf; the cow is crossing over to the other side of the road. I'm not concerned at this point, but I do command the dogs to keep on going, telling them, "On by, on by." All of a sudden the massive mother cow is running beside us! I am thinking, "Oh my, look at the size of this animal!" The cow then runs up ahead of us and blocks the trail. Terror-stricken, the leaders stop and begin to back up. I panic, jumping off the four-wheeler. The cow then lifts herself up and pounces on the dogs, pounding two in rapid fire on the head with her front hooves.

"Oh my God," I whisper, eyes widened in terror.

The team is bunching up to avoid being hit by the cow's kicking, stomping hooves, as she picks herself up again and comes down on the team. I look at the cow. Our eyes connect. She charges after me! I bolt away from the scene as fast as possible. The going is harder, and I look over my shoulder to see if the cow is coming after me. She is right behind me! My legs begin to weaken. I'm telling myself, "She is going to catch up to me if I don't get off the trail." I am thinking this is my last day on earth. Reflexively, I dart sharp to the left and start down a hill. I grab hold of two trees. I stop there and begin to pray. I ask God for mercy and forgiveness. I look back. The moose has stopped. I see her head above the tall bushes. She is looking around. I begin to whisper, "Thank you, God, for your mercy and grace upon me."

It's not over yet, however. The dogs are still on the trail, and I'm not yet back at camp. I begin to run again, watching the bottom of the hill, taking care not to fall. I am walking, running, and looking over my shoulder. I stop to catch my breath. I can hear the team barking in the distance. I don't see the cow anymore, but I am thinking, "Oh no, the team will be seriously hurt or killed if I don't get help soon." I finally sprint to one of the houses in camp and kick off the board holding the door. Inside, I hustle up the stairs, terrified the moose is still close by, stalking me.

I squat down, trying to catch my breath, and attempt to remain calm. I open a window. Flies begin to fall out of the cracks. I wait to stick my head out the window, afraid the flies will drop into my hair or go down my back.

I begin to yell for help, but the camp's electric generator is blaring far too loudly for John to hear me. I estimate it's 100 to 200 yards back to the dog yard. I take a chance, hunched over, and run onto the trail toward the dog yard, where I hear dogs barking. Now it is impossible to hear the team I left behind. I run down another hill and spot John. By now I want to collapse. I'm panting, trying to catch my breath, trying to speak at the same time. My body is shaking and dripping with sweat. John senses immediately there is trouble with the team.

"Get in the truck," he says.

"I can't," I say, still terrified and exhausted.

"Come on. You have to show me where the team is," John explains.

I climb into the back of the truck, finally catching my breath as we drive down the trail to the scene. Despite two dogs being hit by the cow, the team looks okay, all in a straight line and ready to go. The four-wheeler is on the other side of the trail, caught in a bush. I think to myself, "God answered my prayer." I envision angels holding, protecting the front of the team with yet another angel holding the four-wheeler.

"I'll finish running the team around the rest of the trail," John says, and I'm relieved as I climb back into the truck and drive down to the airport, beginning to weep, thanking God again for his mercy and grace.

After settling down, I decide to run the last team, making sure I include our dog lot's most experienced leaders. I sit down on the four-wheeler and take a deep breath.

"Are you ready?" asks John.

"I'm ready," I reply, commanding the team to get ready. "Ok, go ahead," I shout. Observing the sides of the trail, the dogs and I travel smoothly. We slosh through the mud, willows, trees, and tall grass. We make it home safely. I smile and laugh in ecstasy.

We all decide to go up to the main house for coffee and sandwiches. I open up my Bible and read the study verse called "God's Gift," Psalm 51, quote Second Samuel 12:3: "David said to Nathan, 'I have sinned against the Lord.' Nathan replied, 'The Lord also has taken away your sin. You are not going to die.'" Awesome verse!

I guess I should have read my Bible before I did anything else that morning.

IVA MAY BAKER, an Iñupiaq born in 1970, has two Iñupiaq names—
Nunuraq and Ilaguq. She is married to John K. Baker, a well-known top
competitor in Alaska's annual Iditarod Trail Sled Dog Race. They have
two children and live in Kotzebue in northwest Alaska. She says the best
thing about living in rural Alaska is that "less than twenty miles out
of Kotzebue, you can be in the country where there is quietness." She
believes in continuing to learn and grow because "with God, all things
are possible."

R.A. Dillon mushes his dog team on Kotzebue Sound.

4

. . . .

~ KOTZEBUE ~

First sled-dog race offers lessons
R.A. Dillon

JOHN BAKER'S BLUE PARKA was still visible in the distance as I rushed to the front of my team, grabbed the leaders, Rowdy and Gamma, and attempted to straighten a growing tangle of ten dogs.

By the time I straightened the dogs, Baker and five other mushers in the race had disappeared. It didn't matter. Within seconds, my team was snarled again, barely half a mile from the starting line.

I thought of scratching right then. The dogs looked sick; I'd overfed them the night before and now they all had diarrhea. After Rowdy refused to run, Kobuk, who was two dogs back in team position, attacked Rowdy and caused the team to pile up.

I looked Rowdy over. There was no blood, but he seemed shaky. "You don't have to lead, old boy," I told him. "Just keep up until Noatak and then I'll send you home."

I moved Rudy up to lead next to Gamma, put Kobuk in wheel, far from trouble, and decided to push on and see how the dogs did—at least as far as the portage, twenty-five miles up the Noatak River. I had lost an hour. We made good time to the portage, averaging almost twelve miles per hour. Maintaining the same pace, I could reach Noatak within a couple hours of the leaders.

Snow cover on the portage was thin, with frozen tussocks the size of a man's head jutting out of the tundra, making travel hazardous. The sled's runners slipped into crevices between the mounds, then bounced out again. My feet were in constant danger of being ripped from the runners. I turned the toes of my boots in toward the center of the sled and tightened my grasp on the driving bow. Once on top of the five-mile portage trail, though, the trail smoothed out and the scenery took over. The white tips of the Igichuk Hills glowed pink from the setting sun. My confidence returned and I decided to push on to Noatak. I hoped to catch the back of the pack while they snacked their teams at the shelter cabin just ahead. I watched for the trail to veer off to the right toward where I believed the shelter cabin should be. But the trail kept to the left side of the river, and I saw no sign of any resting teams. As darkness descended, I realized the other teams weren't stopping to rest. They were sprinting to Noatak, something my team was not trained to do. I had no hope of catching up, and was too far down the trail to turn around.

Rowdy's tug was slack again, but he had helped pull over the portage and was still keeping up with the team. Gamma and Rudy looked confident in double lead. The rest of the team was tired, but determined. Our speed had dropped to eight miles per hour, and we were only halfway through the first leg of the race.

At least I thought we were halfway to Noatak. At the prerace meeting, race official Dan Snyder said the race would follow the river all the way because of the lack of snow covering the Noatak flats.

The normal trail measures about sixty-two miles, but no one knew exactly how many extra miles would be added by following the winding river. As a group, we guessed about eight. But as early evening turned into night, I realized Noatak was much farther than that. I could feel the team slowing down. We were no longer racing. We were marching.

I hadn't run the dogs more than fifty miles in training. Rudy, a young male who loves running up front, looked over his shoulder to make sure I wanted to continue.

I never had run my dogs more than fifty miles during training. Rudy, an eighteen-month-old male who loved to run up front, was looking over his shoulder constantly, checking to make sure I really wanted to keep going.

"It's time to turn around and head home," his looks told me. I replaced Rudy in lead and we fumbled on.

The temperature in Kotzebue at the start of the race was 5 below zero. As we followed the trail off the main river and down a twisting channel, the temperature plummeted to 46 below. The dogs and I had no idea we were headed toward the coldest spot in the country that day.

In addition to the cold, which crawled across my parka looking for gaps and slithered around my toes, steam wafted off open water on the river. The steam swallowed us like a fog, dampening everything that went through it.

I turned on my headlamp to locate the open lead in the river, but the light was weak. I could see only the wheel dogs. I shook the battery pack to see if I could wring out any more power. The light flickered out.

At least the dogs were staying on the trail, plodding through the darkness. Noatak had to be close.

It was already after nine o'clock. I had been on the trail more than nine hours, four of them in the dark. Noatak would emerge like Bethlehem, bright and warm, just around the next corner, I thought. I stopped reluctantly for the third time and snacked the dogs. Half the team curled up into balls in the snow; the other half wolfed down their sheefish and tried to steal from anyone who wouldn't eat.

I rifled through my sled bag and pulled out every spare piece of clothing I had. When I was done, I hardly could move my head and arms from all the layers of clothes.

I gave the "ready" command and watched the dogs wobble to their feet. "Alright," I said, and somehow, they found the strength to stagger forward.

I knew I was so far behind that there was a good chance I had been forgotten. I had not seen a snowmachine since the portage and now my mind was starting to play tricks on me in the darkness. I had expected the race to be fast, had expected to feed the dogs extra food, and I had expected to be in last place. But I had not expected to be scared of the dark.

I changed the batteries in my headlamp, but they had been zapped by the cold and offered only a weak beam. Now, as the dogs crawled forward, I knew I was depending on them for survival.

I realized I knew nothing about arctic survival. Should I stop and climb into my sled bag and sleeping bag for warmth? Should I try to start a fire? As a journalist, how many stories had I written about people who had frozen to death after breaking through the ice?

While I fell apart, the dogs kept moving. I held on and prayed for a snowmachine to pass by.

At long last, a light flashed. I thought I was hallucinating. Then I realized the flickering in the distance was an airport beacon. Noatak had to be straight ahead. I wiped my eyes and started to kick behind the sled. The dogs sensed my interest and picked up the pace. Noatak was still miles away—disappearing with a bend in the river and reappearing an hour later—but at least I knew for sure something was out there. As we ran below the lights of the town, the dogs broke into a full run. Every dog in Noatak announced our arrival.

I parked the team outside the high school and stumbled into the empty gymnasium. My watch said quarter 'til midnight. It had taken us almost twelve hours to travel seventy-eight miles.

"I've been looking for you," Elmer Howarth said a moment later. "I went down the trail about twenty miles but never saw you."

I smiled. I hadn't been forgotten. "I was looking for you, too," I replied.

That night, I slept in the Howarths' living room. Rowdy curled up in the kitchen next to the warm stove. Kathy Howarth fed her visitors roasted chicken and mashed potatoes until we almost burst.

The next morning I scratched. I sent Rowdy home with race officials, his body sick and badly frostbitten, and followed the last musher out of Noatak with nine dogs.

The dogs seemed disappointed five hours later when I was met with a snowmachine and dog box ten miles from the portage on the Noatak side. They seemed determined to make it on their own. Perhaps they know something I still have to learn.

ROBERT A. DILLON, who goes by "Dillon," was born in 1969 and has worked as a photographer and reporter for newspapers, magazines, and radio stations in the Czech Republic, Russia, Austria, China, and the United States. Dillon spent six years as a newspaper editor and reporter documenting the lives of Yup'ik and Iñupiaq Eskimos in Alaska in both Kotzebue and Bethel. In 2004, he returned to the Czech Republic to run Spectrum Pictures, a photo agency specializing in Eastern Europe. He was also business editor at the Prague Post. He later returned to Alaska as a reporter for the *Fairbanks Daily News-Miner,* then in 2006 moved to the East Coast. In 2010, he was working on the staff of Alaska Senator Lisa Murkowski as a spokesman on energy issues.

Nancy Berkey worried about her son Keith, a U.S. Marine,
above, when he served his country in Afghanistan after 9/11.

5

. . . .

~ THORNE BAY ~

The graying of my hair
Nancy Berkey

I BLAME THE GRAYING OF MY HAIR on my son Keith, starting with his conception. I was told by three doctors that I'd die from another pregnancy, but they didn't mention the hardship of actually rearing another child.

Early on, all signs pointed to pregnancy, but I tried to ignore them until the doctor confirmed my worst fears. At age twenty-eight, I started to sprout gray hair.

When Keith's day came to enter the world, my doctor regarded my three previous problem deliveries as an opportunity to train an internist on difficult births. Giving birth is stressful enough without having to wonder whether an inexperienced intern was going to kill my baby.

After little Keith's head emerged, his shoulders, unfortunately, did not come through like a normal delivery, so the attending nurses placed their hands on top of my abdomen and thrust down on me with every contraction.

After more pains, pushes, and prayers, Keith was born, weighing nine pounds, five ounces, and nineteen inches long. The stress of his birth, though, caused his heart to beat irregularly. Two nurses whisked our little boy to the other side of the room and placed him on a table. They suctioned his nostrils and mouth and tried to get him to breathe. Fortunately, they succeeded, though it seemed an eternity before his blue body started to pink up. Keith was kept in intensive care for twenty-four hours.

He eventually did pull out of danger, and we left the hospital three days later, but that didn't stop his mother's gray hairs from spreading.

Keith and I had to stay in Ketchikan for a few more days before returning home to Naukati, a logging camp on Prince of Wales Island in southeast Alaska. During that time I had acquired not a few gray hairs but a streak that had not existed just a few weeks earlier.

When Keith was nine months old, life intensified. He was walking a little and was a quick crawler. On a visit to his paternal grandmother's house, he grabbed for the fruit bowl and managed to retrieve a prune from the bowl and swallow it before I could do anything. The pit stuck in his throat. I was unable to see it or even feel it. Keith struggled to breathe as I tried to dislodge the pit.

As I raced to the only radiophone in camp (which had no telephones), I said a silent prayer. The pit finally went down.

Life then passed a bit more peacefully, but only until my angel turned fifteen months. By then, little Keith could scale walls. My other children had not prepared me for this child.

One time Keith tried to take my hair-spray pump bottle apart to drink the contents. I finally removed the contents and gave him the bottle. Much to my chagrin, he did not care about the bottle. He wanted the contents, and he had watched where I put the hair spray. While I was helping one of the other children, he snitched it and quickly guzzled some. This first call to poison control was followed by many more, and all these calls were made by my husband Mike, Keith's father, a licensed amateur radio operator.

One day, Keith crawled up onto his sister's chair and was eating the cereal she had left. I had my back turned, washing dishes. As Mike walked past Keith, Mike could see that his son was choking on the corn flakes. Keith's lips had turned blue. Acting quickly, Mike pulled the corn flakes from Keith's throat. Luckily, Keith started breathing again. I was mortified. My son could have died as I washed the dishes.

A few weeks later, while I was mopping the kitchen floor, Keith drank some of the mop water. He was supposed to be taking his nap, not sneaking up behind me. He had managed to get a cup, dip it into the mop bucket that contained a high concentration of bleach and water, and drink some.

My husband called poison control again. This time, when he got on frequency, a radio operator who was listening in said, "We need to take that boy away from that family. That's child abuse." At that particular time, I felt like replying, "Fella, if you want him, you can have him!"

Keith had to drink lots of water for his treatment, and we were to watch for blisters that might develop in his mouth and throat. Luckily, only one blister developed. I don't know what we would have done if there had been more, because we lived forty-five minutes by air from the nearest hospital. On that particular day, the weather was bad with low visibility and high-wind warnings. Our community had no medical airlift services in those days.

My husband called poison control again. When he got on frequency, a radio operator listening in said, "We need to take that boy away from that family. That's child abuse."

After a few more close calls, Keith moved on to a markedly less hazardous life, but not before his mother started longing for Miss Clairol.

Not long after one of these near-death escapades, a small floatplane landed in Naukati after dark. The camp superintendent simply assumed Keith was in trouble again and that the plane had flown in for a quick med-evac. The superintendent rushed over to our house. Out of breath, the man inquired about what happened to Keith. "Is he all right?" he asked.

"Yes, Keith is all right," I assured him, realizing that Keith had traumatized others in Naukati, not just his parents!

I endured more graying of my hair in the ensuing years, but most of it already had turned silver before this child had turned two.

NANCY G. BERKEY, born in 1950, lives in Sedro Woolley, Washington, where she teaches reading at the Cascades Job Corps Center. Of Nez Perce and Sioux descent, she and her husband raised their three sons and one daughter in rural Alaska and have six grandchildren. She holds a bachelor's degree in elementary education, an endorsement in reading, and hopes to complete a master of education degree. Among the subsistence delicacies she has enjoyed are venison, seafood, berries, and kelp pickles. She says one of rural Alaska's best attributes centers on "the need for the community to work as a whole."

A charter boat arrives at Craig, Alaska.

6

. . . .

A well-oiled crew in harrowing waters
Marcus Miller

WITHOUT WARNING, THE CAPTAIN threw the helm hard over to starboard. Instinctively, he steered to avoid what appeared to be a reef barely visible in the stormy, confused seas. The big fishing boat rolled on her beam ends and began a broaching motion in the trough, parallel to the waves. This 104-foot ex-navy, World War II-vintage craft was designed for open-sea rescue operations along with a crew of experienced sailors. We were a green crew—three idealists bound for Alaska's rich fishing grounds.

Our voyage had begun in Seattle. We were headed for Craig, a fishing village on Prince of Wales Island at the southernmost tip of southeast Alaska.

Caught parallel between the waves, the side-to-side motion forced Captain Bill to clamp his large hands onto the wheel and brace himself against the pedestal-mounted chair as he made a desperate attempt to steer out of the trough. I tightened my grip on the radar screen eyepiece while trying to maintain my footing. The boat, nearly out of control, was forcing us to handle the crisis quickly. For a fleeting second, I wondered if the boat would right herself if she rolled over.

Reflecting back decades later to this ordeal in April of 1971, I know that we should have known better that morning, as we pulled out of a sheltered bay at the northern tip of Vancouver Island in British Columbia. The weather forecast from Canadian Marine Radio called for storm warnings, including sixty-knot winds and seas to fifteen feet. We expected a three- or four-day trip to make our first port in Ketchikan. We worried about crossing Queen Charlotte Sound as sea conditions deteriorated, but we sailed ahead anyway.

"I hope we can make the Inside Passage before this gets any worse," said the captain.

The storm, however, continued to worsen as the wild seas smashed into the bow. The wind blew spume off the crests of the waves, splattering on the windshield like pellets from a shotgun blast. I remember thinking that with a little luck, we could maintain this course and should have a safe passage. Hour after hour, the bow crashed ominously into the oncoming sea, staggered for a moment on the crest, then surfed rapidly down into the trough. The motors were struggling to maintain control as the next wave met us head on.

The captain, withdrawn and silent, told us without words that he was worried. He had been up the entire time and was determined to remain so until the storm eased. We motored on into the evening while the wind-driven rain obscured all but a few feet of our forward visibility. Jim, the third member of the crew, was below, off watch, trying to get some much-needed sleep. I had buried my face in the rubber eyepiece that surrounded the radar screen up until the moment our fate plunged from bad to worse.

Our fate went from bad to worse. At one point, the cupboard doors and drawers suddenly flew open, spilling our supplies onto the floor. "Secure the galley!" the captain yelled.

At one point, the cupboard doors and drawers suddenly flew open in the galley, spilling our supplies onto the floor.

"Secure the galley!" the captain yelled over the noise.

Obediently, I charged through the companionway and immediately joined the chaos that was unfolding before me. With no handholds to grab, I slipped on the floor, down with the pots and pans. While it had been nearly impossible to keep the boat's supplies from thrashing around the galley, it instantly became hopeless after a gallon of vegetable oil splattered its slippery contents onto the deck.

At the same time, Jim came flying out of his bunk after an unexpected change of the boat's course and rushed into the galley. He slipped, skating across the oil-slick floor, and scored like a human hockey puck a "goal" between the upright legs of the galley table. Time and again, Jim and I fell over each other, trying to regain our footing as the boat flopped from side to side.

Finally, the captain managed to get the vessel under control, and we got the galley back in order. Still dripping in oil and slightly hysterical, Jim and I reverted quickly back to our routine. We knew better than to test the skipper's humor this time.

It took three days to make that crossing. The wind never let up. We spent the final evening fighting the choppy water of Dixon Entrance, waiting for daylight, before pushing on to Ketchikan.

After tying up at Ketchikan's public dock, Jim and I jumped onto shore. Waddling like ducks, we anticipated a heaving deck meeting our feet, but the ground was stationary. All we had to do was find it.

Glad to be intact, with a seaworthy tale to tell, we headed for the city lights with a new meaning for the term, "a well-oiled crew."

MARCUS R. MILLER, born in 1947, lives in Haines in southeast Alaska. In addition to being a retired teacher, mostly having worked in the rural Iditarod Area School District, he has commercial-fished and worked as an airplane mechanic. He holds a bachelor of science degree in industrial arts education. In 2010, he was employed part-time as a woodworker and continued to fish his commercial salmon troller during the "nice time" of the year. He is married to Beverly Schupp, also a retired teacher, and artist.

Kotzebue plows remove massive piles of snow
after back-to-back blizzards in 2009.

7

. . . .

~ KOTZEBUE ~

Minnesotan respects Kotzebue cold
Karl Puckett

EVER SINCE I WAS A KID, I had been reveling in all those tough winter-weather things favored by "cold enough for ya?" Minnesotans.

I fished on frozen lakes. I walked to school every day no matter the temperature, no matter the snow depth. I played hockey and broomball on Minnesota's outdoor rinks, enduring cheek-chafing wind-chills and toe-numbing temperatures.

Despite those experiences, Kotzebue's spit-freezing temperatures and house-swaying blizzards humbled me in this remote settlement I once called home, twenty-six miles above the Arctic Circle in northwest Alaska. I no longer partake in the cold-weather bravado of Minnesotans—not after watching people in the arctic embark on sixty- or seventy-mile snowmobile trips across the tundra the same way Minnesotans hop into their four-by-fours for trips to the convenience store up the road. Not after seeing head-high snow banks line Kotzebue's narrow roads. Not after witnessing monster snowdrifts still standing proud and tall well into May.

My wife and I moved to treeless Kotzebue in 1989 to run the local newspaper, *The Arctic Sounder*. The town sits on the tip of a tiny sliver of a peninsula that juts into the Chukchi Sea. I swear I could toss a baseball to a Russian if Kotzebue's notorious winter winds were blowing in the right direction.

Like an overbearing party guest, winter comes early and

stays late in the arctic. By the third week of September, local commercial fishermen barely had pulled in their nets from Kotzebue Sound before winter's first huge, watery flakes speckled the puddled dirt outside our door. I remember watching what seemed like waffle-sized flakes float to the earth.

To me, September always says fall football—the Minnesota Vikings. But damned if it wasn't snowing in Kotzebue by early fall.

Kotzebue's first full-blown blizzard of the season blasted through town on November 10, followed by a second howler a week later. At least six or seven more three-day-whiteout wonders ripped through Kotzebue after that, and that doesn't count the less severe, if more frequent, arctic squalls that would be considered to be truly nasty weather in Minnesota.

I swear I could toss a baseball to Russia if Kotzebue's notorious winter winds blew in the right direction. Like an overbearing party guest, winter comes early and stays late.

Oh, sure, Minnesota spits some ornery blizzards, but usually only one or two potent ones a winter. They hardly compare to these brawling beasts of the arctic. Trees help to blunt the wind in the Twin Cities, but the only trees I'd ever seen in Kotzebue were some scrawny, over-priced twigs shipped from down south for the Christmas season. The lack of wind-blunting trees means that everything in town—dogs, houses sitting on stilts atop the permafrost, cars—gets buried by blizzards.

In fact, the sled-dog team that lived next door to us would vanish in these storms. The huskies would curl up, burrow in, and allow the snow to drift over them until they disappeared. A local friend told a story about a dog that entered its hut for cover at the beginning of an arctic blizzard and was buried alive.

At first, I thought these blizzards were neat, especially the way we had to tunnel ourselves through the sloping drift that barricaded our door after every big blow. I've shoveled my share of driveways in Minnesota, but nothing compares to pitching the white stuff up here. Ever shovel concrete?

The winds are what make Kotzebue winters truly wicked, particularly when combined with below-zero temperatures that are as common as lost snowmachiners and roving dog packs.

I wasn't used to frost forming on my nose hairs, eyebrows and what little mustache and stubble I have on my smooth Nordic face during the short walk to work. I wasn't used to dressing as if I intended to walk to the North Pole every day. I wasn't used to donning more than $700 worth of cold-weather gear for the march to work.

Despite the utter cold that humbled the Minnesotan in me, it was the arctic winter's length and breadth that stunned me.

By October of my first arctic winter, for instance, Kotzebue already was averaging just 24 degrees, according to the National Weather Service. That dipped to 4 below zero in November. By early November, I had shed my fall attire to strap on the winter armor, as the locals—mostly Iñupiaq Eskimos—continued to zip around town on four-wheelers and snowmachines wearing baseball caps and sneakers. The average monthly temperature didn't creep out of the below-zero range until well into April, when it warmed to an average of 14 degrees.

On February 6, Kotzebue hit 49 below. Between February 3 and February 9, the temperature never rose above 30 below, which is considered cold even by local standards. At those temperatures, ice fog makes travel outside even more dangerous than usual. In good weather, when visibility stretches at least a quarter of a mile, screaming snowmachines streak within inches of local pedestrians, who cling to the margins of Kotzebue's skinny, snow-packed gravel roads, which are uselessly posted with speed limit signs of ten or fifteen miles per hour. When shrouded in ice fog, the chance of becoming roadkill quadruples.

On one of those 30-below days, I surprised myself when I was able to cajole a dilapidated hunk of steel, our Jeep, to life with the help of a battery charger. As I was congratulating myself for venturing outside that day, I noticed local people going about their business as if it were one of those June days when the arctic is blessed with twenty-four hours of sunlight.

In Minnesota, I rarely wore a hat during winter. In Kotzebue, a rare winter's day passed without my head firmly ensconced in a silver fox hat, its bushy tail dangling down my back. In Minnesota, I wore a wool coat that covered me neck to waist. In Kotzebue, my parka hung over my thighs and sported a hood that looked like one of those ancient, deep-sea-diving bubble helmets.

In Minnesota I slipped around on "boat shoes" or sneakers. Kotzebue winters found me plodding about in a $120 pair of calf-high boots that could squash a small dog, but ah, them suckers is guaranteed to keep my size tens warm to 85 below.

Temperatures never reached 85 below in Kotzebue that winter—unless, of course, you're taking into account wind-chill factor. In any case, for this "cold-enough-for-ya?" Minnesotan, it was cold enough for me in Kotzebue.

It was May when I wrote this. At least that's what the calendar had said. Ha! At least thirty inches of snowpack and massive drifts still covered the ground in Kotzebue.

Good grief. I was playing tennis in Minnesota in May.

Afterword

It would take two decades before the infamous winter of 1988-89 was equaled. In a town that almost never shuts down for weather, government agencies, and businesses closed repeatedly over several weeks as one ferocious arctic blizzard after another blasted Kotzebue during the 2008-09 winter season. Local elders said 2008-09 resembled winters of their youth, when snow would amass in huge drifts around town.

Winter storms caused several deaths, including two snow-machiners caught in a whiteout on their way to Kotzebue from village upriver. A Kiana woman who disappeared on the streets of Kotzebue was found frozen to death two days later on the ice outside of town.

KARL PUCKETT, born in 1964, grew up in Minnesota, where he served as the community editor of the Brooklyn Park *Sun-Post,* a weekly newspaper near Minneapolis. In 2010, he was working as a reporter covering natural resources for the *Great Falls Tribune* in Montana. He is a former reporter at *The Arctic Sounder*, a weekly newspaper that serves Alaska's Northwest Arctic and North Slope boroughs.

Burton Haviland Jr. and, from left, daughters Desiree
and Shawna and wife Kimberly in 2005

8
. . . .

~ KOTZEBUE ~

The long road to recovery
Burton W. Haviland Jr.

I FIRST DRANK ALCOHOL when I was five.

In those days, I lived with my family in a small two-bedroom house next to Rotman's store on Front Street in my hometown of Kotzebue. With no running water, my parents hauled water for drinking and running the household, and that's how I first tasted alcohol. One day, they had forgotten to get water before a party. Consequently, a thirsty buddy and I had no water to drink the following morning. We discovered some glasses on the table, however, with clear liquid in them. We quenched our thirst.

My grandfather, *Ataata* Leslie later told me that we came laughing and stumbling drunk into his home that morning. Grandpa Leslie put us down to sleep it off. About two years later, my two youngest brothers would repeat this same experience. Alcohol seemed to be a normal part of growing up.

Yet, like innocent five-year-olds anywhere, I experienced happiness in birthdays; Christmas trees that sparkled and twinkled with multicolored lights and tinsel; Independence Day skies that exploded with the crackle of fireworks in the midnight sun; and each Halloween when we little, colorful monsters shuffled door to door under a crisp moon seeking sweet treasures. A common thread wove itself through all our years of growing up, though, and that thread was alcohol.

For me, alcohol eventually would become a devastating addiction, along with other recreational drugs, and I would continue to fight this battle for years amid nearly unbearable pain. This is my story of a spiraling descent into the insanity and helplessness of addiction. It also is the story of my recovery—one that I hope and pray will continue for the rest of my life.

During those early days, in my child's mind, the grownups around me drank a strong-smelling liquid that came in tall brown bottles and brightly colored cans. When my parents and their friends and relatives drank at home, they laughed and joked through many seemingly endless nights. I don't know what my parents did when they ventured over to their friends' homes, as they did frequently, but I assumed it was more of the same.

A typical evening of adult fun began with my parents donning elegant clothes. My mother put on silky-looking dresses and high-heeled shoes. Friends would spray and primp her hair until it became big, smooth, and shiny. My father dressed in handsome gray or blue suits with black shoes so polished you could almost see your reflection in them. The young sitter (usually a cousin) would arrive, and Mom and Dad would leave for the evening. When they returned late at night, sometimes with friends or relatives, glassy-eyed and happy, invariably they made enough noise to awaken one or more of us children.

They gesticulated with grandiose animation as they spoke, laughed great belly laughs, told jokes incomprehensible to my child's mind, and generally appeared to be enjoying themselves— but not always. Occasionally, hopeless crying replaced gay laughter, and violent yelling replaced light-hearted joking.

"Feed the kids!" seemed to be a recurring war cry from my father.

My mother generally replied with vicious profanity, or she threw things. I couldn't see the point of all that; I don't remember being hungry at those particular times. Through it all, my brothers, little sister, and I didn't pay too much attention. We grew up with these sorts of events as a part of normal life, although today I realize that not everyone grows up this way.

Eventually my parents would find the peace and happiness of sobriety themselves, though their marriage didn't withstand the rigors of time or their own growth in different directions.

Later in life, they have numbered among my most trusted advisors and friends, proving invaluable in my own personal growth into manhood.

One morning when I was four, I awoke to an empty house strewn with broken and scattered dishes. No one was around. I didn't even consider it out of the ordinary that the house was in disarray, or that I was alone. I had begun looking after myself, and, later, so would my younger siblings.

I quickly got bored and lonely, so I dressed and made my way to Grandpa Leslie's home down Front Street, where he lived with other members of my extended family; I knew Grandpa always would take me in. There always seemed to be an uncle or two living with *Ataata* Leslie; they looked after me, too.

At the same time, unfortunately, several adults, but one in particular, perpetuated acts of an unspeakable form of abuse done to children. Without going into detail, I'll just say the experience left me ashamed of the most intimate aspect of myself and emotionally unable to initiate normal interaction with girls my age.

In elementary school, I avoided a female classmate who I thought was cute. Not knowing the nature of what I was feeling, I felt anger and dislike for her. Whenever I saw her approaching, I cringed. Sometimes I turned and walked the other way.

During much of my life, I have felt uncomfortable around girls and women I found attractive. The inability to express myself in that area, or even simply to introduce myself to a member of the opposite sex, caused emotional conflict.

One evening in Kotzebue, at about age of twelve, as a friend and I were walking home just before curfew, a girl I found very attractive approached us going home in the opposite direction.

"She's beautiful," I said to my pal.

"Well, stop her and talk to her. See if she'll go out with you," he replied, egging me on with an insistent nod.

"OK," I said, although the thought almost made me panic.

"Hi!" I said as I tried to get in front of her.

"Hi," she said, as she stepped around me without missing a beat.

"Where are you going?" I asked of her back.

"Home, of course!" said her back.

My heart sank with shame and embarrassment.

I didn't approach another attractive girl or woman, at least while I was sober, for the next eighteen years. I stayed passive and allowed them to make the initial advance.

One summer, near the end of high school, when I was sixteen, a young woman, age nineteen, who had graduated high school the previous year, took me as her boyfriend. She took me home with her one evening and showed me pleasure that I didn't know was possible; I fell in love instantly.

Looking back across the clarity of time, I can see that, emotionally, I was ill-equipped to hold up my end of a healthy relationship. I was unable to trust my girlfriend fully because, unconsciously, I could not believe that any woman would continue to desire me and remain faithful if she knew me as I saw myself—a shameful creature, somewhat less than human. When I was four, I was made to believe that I should never feel good about my sexuality and that having people see that part of myself was the worst thing that could happen to a human being. Exposure was a horror to be feared and avoided at all cost.

Nevertheless, I was able to be a faithful and attentive partner to my girlfriend, although I became jealous and controlling. I had to know where she was and what she was thinking, at all times. In this way, I could be sure that I would not have to compete with other men for her love, a competition I was sure I could not win. I've learned, over many painful years since, that true love is something given freely, not won in competition. That misconception nearly drove me to suicide.

After I graduated from high school in 1981, my girlfriend and I decided to go to college together at the University of Alaska Fairbanks. Until then, I had drunk alcohol a few times on special occasions, but nothing more. But on Halloween in Fairbanks that fall, my girlfriend and I went to the campus bar, where I guzzled several pitchers of beer to her one. Apart from my early childhood experience, this was the first time I'd ever consumed enough alcohol to get drunk.

As I drank more beer, I began to feel warm and comfortable,

a feeling unknown to me until that night. I let my guard down. I danced with my girlfriend with no discomfort. I had danced with her and others many times before, but that day I realized I had been an exhibitionist, trying to draw attention away from the fact that I was ashamed of myself by putting on a somewhat outrageous act of self-confidence.

I liked the wondrous feeling of euphoria and pleasure that alcohol gave me that night. My girlfriend and I returned to Kotzebue for Christmas vacation, but I decided not to return to school. I felt demoralized not being able to keep up with my studies and had no direction and ambition. My girlfriend returned to school, but only after I extracted a promise of fidelity from her. Coercing that promise must have been the last childish act my girlfriend could take from me. Not long after she returned to Fairbanks, I received a letter.

"I found your last letter cute, but I've decided that I can no longer continue our relationship," she wrote. "So I'm ending it now."

I could not believe it. I thought that I was the center of her universe. I thought she could not possibly exist without me, a budding alcoholic at nineteen. I was not emotionally equipped to accept, much less mature from, the experience. For the first time in my life, I felt profound loss and remorse so strong I thought I would go insane. So, I did what many young men might do: I immediately found myself a new long-term relationship.

With alcohol.

Alcohol soothed the pain nicely. Alcohol allowed me to be the kind of person I wanted to be. When I drank, I could deal with the emotional trauma of lost love. Alcohol made me outgoing, enthusiastic, sociable, charismatic, even a better musician.

Only later would I learn that alcoholics share similar sentiments the world over.

"What a wonderful thing was this alcohol! Why hadn't I discovered it long before?" wrote Bill Wilson, one of the authors of the book, *Alcoholics Anonymous*, which I would read many years later.

At this point, alcohol was becoming my best friend, my confidante; it fueled my fun and helped me to make new friends. After three or four years, though, my tolerance for alcohol began to drop, and I began to face trouble socially. Some embarrassing lapses in judgment about my rapidly descending lifestyle led to shouting matches with my parents, with whom I still lived. I brawled with my brothers and with my friends.

One time, two brothers, a friend, and I purchased a bottle of 151-proof rum from a Kotzebue bootlegger. We walked to the bridge that runs over the entrance of the boat harbor. At the time, I was hobbling around on crutches after spraining an ankle during an alcohol-related blackout. (How my ankle had been injured, I still don't know.)

"Does anyone have a chaser?" I asked.

"Nope," they answered in chorus.

"That's OK," I said. "We'll just have to take straight shots."

We passed the bottle around several times. After about half an hour of that routine, I blacked out. The next thing I remember was waking up in my bed in my parents' home the following day. By then, I had come to consider blackouts normal, something that happened to everyone—except this time I awoke in wet clothes.

"What the...why am I wet?" I thought, as I got up and went downstairs for coffee, "and where are my crutches?"

One of my brothers had a deep, pink gash over one eye.

"What happened to your eye?" I asked, though I didn't want to hear his answer.

"You don't remember?" he asked, straightening up a little, looking at me with disgust.

"No..." I replied, bracing myself.

"You started hitting me and our brother with your crutches," he explained. "We had to gang up and throw you off the bridge." By now, anger was spreading over his face and intensifying in his voice.

That explained the wet clothes.

"I'm sorry."

That's all I could say through a cloud of shame. Somehow, though, saying I was sorry only further cheapened the deed, because saying that you are sorry for doing a thing implies that you won't do it again. But there was no way for me to make that guarantee as long as I kept drinking. The conflict between my apology and reality of my behavior became a problem that eventually touched almost everyone I knew.

My brother did not dignify my apology with an answer. We only spoke a handful of words to each other in the next week or so. (Fortunately, though, he eventually forgave me.)

During those hazy days, I had begun a new relationship with a local woman, someone who liked to drink as much, actually more, than I did. We spent many tender moments guzzling booze, seeking relief from life at the bottom of a bottle. Then, because of my diminished alcohol tolerance and sloppy social behavior, I decided that drinking was not for me anymore; it was not worth it.

I quit drinking forever.

That is, until the following weekend. Then I'd be invited to still another drinking party and would start the cycle all over again. I did make several abortive attempts to quit by personal resolutions, promises to my new girlfriend, and attempts to control when and how much I drank, but I never succeeded. Eventually, I convinced myself that I really did want to keep drinking.

The truth? I was hopelessly addicted to alcohol.

My girlfriend and I continued to drink this way for five and a half years, during which time our two daughters were born. We built a ruinously unfaithful and stormy relationship. Infidelity was an ongoing problem for both of us.

If I had my moments of swearing off drinking until the next party, so did she. Her life, too, had been filled with both the pain of abuse as a child, as well as with the suffering of being an adult alcoholic. She had lost her first daughters from a previous relationship to the state of Alaska, due to drinking.

"I'm going to get custody of my two daughters. I'm going to quit drinking and if you want to be with us, you'll have to quit too," my girlfriend told me.

After considering her ultimatum for about two seconds, I bolted out the door for another drinking party. Nothing was going to get between alcohol and me.

My girlfriend showed up at the party later that night. But

I'd already met another woman and become intimate with her right away; I told my ex I would not take her back. This lasted a couple of days until the other woman left me, but not before my girlfriend had outdone me in the number of lovers she took to avenge my scorn of her. This pattern continued throughout our relationship.

I was unable to end that relationship permanently until much later. I learned painfully that we had become, in addiction jargon, "codependent." We served each other by perpetuating one another's alcoholism. My self-esteem sank so low that I thought she was the only one who could want me. I kept returning to the relationship, even though I no longer wanted to be with her, with us both unable to change.

Eventually I could not bear the shame of my part in such a destructive relationship. I took my older daughter to Anchorage from Kotzebue to get away from my significant other, leaving my younger daughter in the care of my mother. A few days after I arrived in Anchorage, though, my mother informed me that my younger daughter was in the custody of the state of Alaska. My ex-girlfriend had brought our nine-month-old daughter to Anchorage and had left her in a hotel room, then taken a taxi downtown to hit the bars. The police intervened after other hotel guests reported a baby crying for hours.

Eventually I lost custody of my older daughter, too, due to my own run-in with the law. I had left her with her mother and her mother's new boyfriend overnight at their Anchorage apartment after Thanksgiving dinner in 1992. I returned later that night, drunk. They wouldn't let me in, so I broke their windows out of anger.

That resulted in a vandalism charge, which the state Division of Family and Youth Services (now called the Office of Children's Services) used to gain custody of my older daughter, too. The state cited bad judgment on my part for leaving my older daughter with a person who was a danger to the child and expressed concern that I, too, was a danger to my daughter. Looking back with a sober mind's eye, I have to agree with the state of Alaska.

The court ordered me to complete a residential alcohol-treatment program before I could get my children back. During this time, their mother never was considered fit to have custody, not even by her own lawyer, despite token appearances in court and many meetings and hearings.

At the time, I was living in Anchorage with my mother, with whom the state had placed my daughters. I was allowed to live with them, but legally I could not be on the premises unless I was sober—a state that continued to diminish for me over time.

I resisted treatment until I had missed my appointment for an assessment of my treatment needs at the Alaska Native Alcoholism Recovery Center (now called the Ernie Turner Center) in Anchorage. I missed it because I had been on a six-day binge, my most intense drinking ever, consuming cheap vodka. I slept after drinking myself to sleep and resumed drinking immediately upon waking up.

Somehow I sobered up. It was a Saturday morning at my ex's trailer. I realized I had missed my appointment for the assessment. I assumed jail was next. I figured I'd never get custody of my daughters. I dragged myself to a bus stop and took a seemingly endless ride home to my mother's trailer, but she already had taken my daughters back to Kotzebue and then to Sisualik, a traditional subsistence camp twelve miles across the water from Kotzebue. She had taken them with her because they were in her care and she wanted to go to camp.

Alone in that hot and muggy trailer, I experienced extreme detoxification as withdrawal overtook my mind, my body, and my soul.

I had hallucinations. Although I was alone in the trailer, I could hear people moving about, opening and closing doors, talking. Multitudes of tiny black insects swarmed around the trailer. When I closed my eyes and tried to sleep, I could still see the room as if my eyes were open, but grotesquely disfigured little people, about twelve inches tall, were running around and getting up on me, bothering me.

I wasn't afraid of seeing things I knew weren't there nor of the terrible nightmares I had when I went to sleep. What scared me first was seeing beyond a doubt that I could not quit drinking, ever. Second, I realized that if I kept drinking, it would kill me in a painful and ugly way. And third, I was going to die drunk.

This realization filled me with a kind of panic I hadn't known until then. I had thought I was prepared to die because I believed that the soul was indestructible and that there was nothing to fear after life. What I feared, I discovered, was living a wasted life; I feared never reaching my full potential.

In that moment, I desperately wanted to live and have a chance to make peace with my creator. I decided, however, there was no such opportunity for atonement, so the best choice was suicide to end my own suffering and that of the people who loved me. Yet, suicide would have left me with the same result—a wasted life. Instead, I decided to seek some sort of divine intervention. With grim determination, I walked the half-mile to the treatment program.

"I've been drinking every day for a week," I told an intake counselor. "I think I damaged my liver because I recently had hepatitis A, and it's swollen up again. I think I'm going to die if I don't stop drinking."

> **The best choice was suicide to end my own suffering and that of the people who loved me. Yet, suicide would have left me with the same result—a wasted life.**

The counselor recommended at least sixty days of in-patient treatment.

I had to consider that for a minute. Sixty days seemed like an awfully long time for a miracle to happen. It didn't occur to me that it might take a while to heal a life ravaged by ten years of hard-core drinking and drugging, but the only alternative was to walk out the door and face prison, insanity, and death—alone.

I learned later that, from the view of twelve-step programs, an addict suffers from a form of insanity that takes away the choice to use or not. It is a habitual behavior that the addict knows will end in pain and death, but is unable to stop unaided. This was the first time since I had become an alcoholic that I'd had that choice.

"OK, what will I need?" I asked.

"Some changes of clothes and a few toiletries," the intake counselor replied. "You have two hours to go and get them and come back, or we won't let you in."

I had to walk past the local liquor stores going to and from the treatment center. For the first time in ten years, it didn't even occur to me to stop for a jug or two. When I returned, they made a bed for me immediately. The first two days were very hard. My hands shook so badly that I barely could hold a cup of the decaffeinated coffee they served. But I did attend group counseling and twelve-step meetings, where I began to learn about my addiction.

A counselor drew an upside-down, bell-shaped curve on a blackboard in a sweltering room on the morning of my third day. He gestured with the chalk, tracing a descending path down the left side.

"Alcoholism can be described as a downward slope," he said. "As alcoholics lose more and more control over their lives, they eventually reach the bottom of the slope and begin a vicious cycle of self-perpetuating abuse."

He made a circular motion with the chalk around the bottom of the curve where he had drawn a spiral.

"If they are not able to seek help, they go around the bottom until they die," he explained. "If they are able to ask for help and start to recover, they begin to climb up the far side of the curve."

He traced a new path, this time ascending the right side of the curve. I felt my interest growing.

"Now we're getting somewhere," I thought.

"In the twelve-step program, the first stop along the way is step one. We admit that we are alcoholic and that our lives have become unmanageable," he said.

The counselor drew a dash a little way up the right side of the curve. I understood that step.

"The next stop on the way up is step two," he continued. "We come to believe that a power greater than ourselves could restore us to sanity." The counselor drew another dash a little higher.

I decided that I'd done that step, too. I already believed in a higher power. I knew that I had some form of fatal mental dysfunction that made me unable to stop drinking.

"The third stop is step three. We make a decision to turn our wills and our lives over to the care of God *as we understand him*," he said.

The moment he said those last words, I realized that I'd never humbled myself enough to ask for help from my higher power. Suddenly I knew I could escape my death sentence. My world became infused with a golden light that shone from everything I could see. A feeling of peace and of excitement rushed through me; in that moment, I asked for help.

"Oh, God, help me!"

That simple, unspoken plea marked the first true prayer I'd ever made, although I'd given lip service to hundreds of half-hearted pleadings for other things in my life.

I knew what I must do. First, I had to quit lying to the people who wanted to help me. That morning, I was scheduled to meet with my primary counselor, a woman about five-foot-ten with dark, shoulder-length. She had a confident, no-nonsense demeanor and a barely perceptible smile that seemed to say, "Whatever your story is, I've heard it before." Her eyes had a twinkle that said, in no uncertain way, "I'll know when you're lying to me."

We began to unravel the twisted rat's nest of lies I'd told to others and to myself throughout my life.

"This is the *real* assessment," she began. "All I'm going to do is go over the assessment questionnaire you filled out when you were admitted. It says here on the question about how much you drink. You answered 'two or three.' Two or three what? Cases? Gallons?"

"That's not really true," I answered. "I really drink about a fifth of liquor a day."

"That sounds more like an alcoholic to me!" she said, her face brightening with enthusiasm.

After some negotiating, we agreed that I consumed one and a half fifths per day on the average. I was amazed. I'd never allowed myself to consider how much I actually drank. I didn't want anyone else to know, either. Yet, there I was, admitting this staggering truth to a stranger.

We continued down the list of questions, correcting numerous outrageous lies, pausing here and there to allow me to elaborate on or clarify the new answers. One of the most eye-opening self-deceptions was my answer to a question of whether I ever became angry. I had written "No." My counselor and I had an incredulous laugh over that one, both shaking our heads in wonder.

"It says here that you have some friends and relatives that have died...?" she asked, indicating the line.

"Yeah, I..."

At that moment, the impact of the deaths of all my loved ones who had died since I started drinking hit me all at once. Their faces all flashed in my memory in quick succession, five or six in all, an abusive adult among them. A heavy dull blow to my chest accompanied the recognition of each face, piercing my soul. I remembered how much I had loved each one of them. I suddenly felt the loss and grief for them that I had denied myself through all those years of drinking.

For the second time in my life, I was devastated with a feeling of loss and grief—so deep and painful—that I stopped breathing. I burst into deep, sobbing tears.

My counselor sat quietly. She knew it was necessary for me to feel the full impact of that pain, without running from it, for healing to begin. For the first time in my life, I felt a release as from a tremendous weight that had been constricting my breath.

There, in that cramped little office, I understood that as long as a person continues to drink, he or she never learns to live with the pain of life. It just stays inside, like a rotting, maggoty corpse. Alcohol is merely a strong perfume, with its own growing stench, that covers the odor.

I completed my treatment plan in sixty-two days, learning a great deal about alcoholism.

The day I got out of treatment, my daughters were returned to me. We stayed at my mother's trailer in Anchorage. Legally, they still were in state custody, but my children's welfare worker believed that I could be trusted. My mother was still at camp at Sisualik.

Several weeks later, my mother and her significant other returned and promptly got drunk, and stayed mostly drunk, for a month. The world seemed to skew a few degrees sideways the first time they walked in the door after having been drinking. I had been depending on them to be my strongest and most sober support system. They had told me that they had quit drinking for good. That living arrangement grew tense and nearly unbearable.

"You guys are alcoholics too!" I yelled at my mother late one night. "I'm gonna take the girls and get my own place!"

"I don't care what you do. This is my home," my mom yelled back. "You put me and our whole family through hell with your drinking. Now look how *you* feel!"

After I calmed down, I realized that I had neither transportation nor any money. I could have asked for outside help, but I feared the state bureaucracy might take my children away from me again.

Meanwhile, I started hanging out with my old drinking buddies, figuring that my desire to stay sober would keep me from relapse. One of those friends came over one night, driving his car after he'd been drinking. He wanted me to drive him around so he wouldn't get another charge of driving while intoxicated. I agreed.

"Where do you want to go?" I asked.

"Let's drive through downtown," he said.

"OK," I replied nonchalantly, heading for downtown Anchorage and its low-quality bars and nightclubs.

"Pull in there," he said, indicating the parking lot of the Hub Bar and Grill.

I knew what was coming next.

"I'll wait for you in the car," I said.

"I'm gonna be in there for a while. Come in with me," he insisted.

I hesitated for fear of the temptation to drink, but the confidence in my sobriety took over. I went in. Surprisingly, I was not tempted to drink. Somehow, the fear of death by alcohol had removed the compulsion to drink, permanently.

That bar had live music with a stunning woman in the house band playing bass guitar, the same instrument I play. I noticed her immediately, but it didn't occur to me to approach her. I was clueless about such things.

While I was in the restroom, my friend asked the bass player to join us during her break. I was amazed to return and see her sitting and talking with my buddy.

Her appearance was everything I had ever wanted in a woman. She stood tall, about five-foot-ten, a large, muscular woman. I later learned that she was a body builder. Her hair fell a little below her shoulders, with shorter, spiked hair on top of her head. Her hair was three different colors: dark blond near the roots, jet-black where it flowed down the back of her neck, and platinum blond for the rest of its length. Green eyes reflected the subdued red, green, and blue lights of the bar.

"Why don't you come back on Tuesday night and jam with the band?" she asked. I accepted.

"Would you like to do something? Maybe eat or catch a movie?" I asked her, after jamming with the band. I was rusty after not having played in a band for several years.

"Sure. I'd like that. Meet me here at closing time tomorrow night."

We went to an all-night coffee shop and talked. We started seeing each other. Ironically, I hung out at bars a lot more in the following five months than I had when I drank.

After a few weeks of seeing her, I discovered that I was in love. This was an amazing discovery for me because, until that moment, I had not believed it possible to love a woman without being intimate with her first. We never did explore that aspect of each other.

During that time, I started hanging out with another friend who had become a crack addict while I was in treatment; before I went in, he was just a heavy drinker. On one occasion, I visited him at the hotel where he was staying; he had asked a mutual friend and me to get some crack for him because I had transportation. I agreed to do it. I still thought I was strong enough not to use.

We were successful.

They went into the bathroom to smoke it while I waited in the outer room. While I was waiting, I was hit with a strong compulsion to smoke with them, but I resisted. Then they asked me to come in and just visit with them while they smoked. I went in, a mistake I would regret for the next six years. When the pipe was passed to me, I could not resist.

"You guys get to see me screw up," I said.

"You're not gonna screw up," they replied. "You just got to control yourself."

They were wrong. That was early in December of 1993. I smoked crack again the following New Year's Eve. At that time, I was attending the aftercare part of my treatment with the Alaska Native Alcohol Recovery Center, going to meetings every week. I decided that those incidents were flukes, not really relapses, so I didn't tell anyone about them, not even my after-care counselor. That was mistake number two.

By the following April, I had gotten legal custody of my kids, but my relationship with the musician fell apart.

"I can't keep staying sober," she told me. "I was under the impression that my life would get better when I quit using, but it just keeps getting worse. Since I don't want you to see me using, and I'm afraid I would hurt you, I'm going to have to stop seeing you."

"Alright, if that's what you want."

That was the only thing there was to say; I really couldn't accept it. I could not believe my higher power would create a world in which two people, who were right for each other, could meet and fall in love, only to have it end before it had really begun, broken by drugs.

About that time, I received my daughters' and my own Alaska Permanent Fund dividends that had been withheld pending disposition of my custody case—about $5,000. I gave a large portion of it to my mother for our bills and food, paid for a used car, got some new clothes and toys for my daughters, and purchased a half-gram of crack. That left $1,900. No problem, I could handle half a gram.

Crack cocaine is a unique drug. The sheer rapidity of its impact, and the equally sudden come-down, combine to create a fierce, unstoppable craving for it. The sudden pleasure of taking a hit of crack is like having an orgasm. But unlike an orgasm, it doesn't stop right away. It goes on as long as fifteen minutes. All the user wants to do is stay in that place. Then, once the drug has run its course through the brain, intense emotional pain sets in.

Over the next month, I whittled away at that $1,900, spending most of it on my new drug of choice, until, to my dismay, the money was gone. I bought anywhere from $20 quarter grams to $80 grams at a time, always making sure to convince myself that this was going to be the last time. Even as I withdrew the last of the money, I convinced myself that it would somehow be replaced. That spring, Mom and her significant other left for camp, leaving me in her trailer again, but this time with my daughters.

The day after my mother left, I pawned her new TV for dope. I told myself that I would get it out of hock within a few days. It stayed in hock and was lost. Later, I pawned her new cordless phone. That was lost too.

A new acquaintance, another addict, became my best friend. He and his girlfriend moved in with us without really asking. He knew that I didn't know where to get dope without the significant risk of being ripped off. I didn't know much about the ways of the crack underworld. He was willing to teach me—for a price. That unspoken price was room and board as well as a share of any crack he bought for me.

"Never sell or give away your pipe. A crackhead without a pipe is useless," my buddy told me one evening after discovering that I didn't have a pipe.

That summer was lonely and frustrating for my daughters. I never left them alone, nor did I leave them with unscrupulous sitters, but they missed me a good part of the time because I either was "stuck" in the bathroom or I retreated to the bedroom for hours on end. In the jargon of crackheads, "stuck" means not being able to put your crack pipe away long enough to do anything else. Another major problem was the inability to buy food—not because I never got enough money to do so, but because I spent nearly every dollar on dope.

"We want juice," my girls informed me one bright afternoon when the temperature was in the 80s.

"We don't have any," I told them.

"We want juice!"

Their three- and four-year-old faces revealed their determination. They were not going to take no for an answer. They had not had nearly as many snacks, juice, or other fun foods as they had been used to getting from their grandmother. I brought home food such as beans, canned salmon, and cheese from food banks. They were angry.

"Fine!" I said as I looked in the refrigerator.

I found a jar of old grape jam. I mixed it with water, and gave it to them. They drank it without complaint, but they did not thank me either.

That incident, among others, defined my disease of crack addiction. Its memory still fills me with remorse and shame. Those two helpless and tiny people were, to me, the most precious beings ever to grace the earth. Yet, I could not buy them a fifteen-cent pack of Kool-Aid and a cup of sugar so they could have juice on a hot day because I hoarded every cent for my drug.

Near the end of summer, my mother called and asked whether I had gotten her TV and cordless phone out of hock yet. I'd admitted to her that I had pawned them, but told her it was for food. I had been promising to get them back after I got $600 in state assistance. I had gotten the money, but I had not retrieved her stuff. I found that I could not keep lying to her, so I told her the truth.

"No I haven't got your stuff out yet. I blew the money on crack. I can't stop smoking it. I need help."

"I'm coming down there to see for myself what's going on," she said with anger and determination in her voice.

When my mother arrived two days later, I was stuck. I could not quit chasing after the next hit of crack long enough to go out to the airport in her van to pick her up as promised. Instead, I piled my kids, a new friend, and the friend's girlfriend into the van and went to another friend's place to hide out, try to get more dope, and continue the party.

By 3 a.m, my children were crying and begging loudly to be taken home. They knew that my mother was there and that she would care for them.

"Just a little while longer, and we'll go home," I kept telling them, until it became clear that there would be no more drugs that night.

"Where have you been?" my mother demanded when I walked into her trailer with my daughters.

"Visiting some friends," I replied.

"Have you been smoking that crack?"

"Yeah, are you going to call the police?" I asked.

"I don't know...I haven't made up my mind yet," she said.

She didn't call the police. Instead, my sister and my mother bought the three of us plane tickets to Kotzebue so I could get away from my situation and try to start over.

In Kotzebue, though, we had nowhere to stay. My younger daughter, my mother, and her boyfriend stayed with a relative, while my older daughter and I stayed at my sister's home. In the meantime, we made improvements to the house I had inherited from *Ataata* Leslie after he died in 1980. I had been renting it to tenants.

After the house was livable, we all moved in. Shortly after that, the Kotzebue senior center offered me a job. I accepted. I had been unemployed for five years, so it was a revelation working in the kitchen, taking care of some custodial duties, and doing some driving. When I received my first paycheck, I had a feeling that, for once in my life, I had some measure of control over my destiny. I paid our bills, bought food, and started paying my mother for her lost possessions.

At my request, my mother and her boyfriend eventually moved out, due to personal differences, around Thanksgiving time in 1994. For the first time in my life, at thirty-one, I was permanently on my own; I knew my family no longer would enable me to keep using drugs by paying my way through life. Usually I was broke by the end of every payday, but we had everything we needed.

Over the next six months, however, I became restless and depressed. On the surface, things were going well. I had received two promotions at work. Yet, the feelings of insecurity and loneliness returned, slithering into the back door of my mind.

Still unable to approach women, the feelings of worthlessness I had carried with me almost my whole life imperceptibly wiggled themselves into every area of my thinking, like weeds growing through cracks in a concrete sidewalk. These seeds of worthlessness were bearing their poisonous fruit.

The emotional pain made me obsess about using. From the moment I awoke in the morning until I struggled to sleep in the wee hours of the following morning, all I could think of was taking a hit.

I started going to twelve-step meetings, but the quality of those meetings in Kotzebue was not adequate at the time. Most if not all of the people who went to the meetings had been ordered to attend by a court. Most were not interested in recovery and had nothing meaningful to say that I could use to help me stay sober.

I was able to stay clean for nine months, but then I relapsed. I tried to find some cocaine, but an old friend took my money and didn't return—a common occurrence. Coke has no friends when it comes to money. Several days later, I was able to find two grams and smoke them, but they had been diluted with filler. In effect, I paid $300 for $40 worth of dope just to get a high going.

That incident angered and frustrated me. I made plans for a Christmas vacation in Anchorage specifically so I could satisfy my craving for cocaine. I would take my children with me. I planned to drop the girls off with my mother, who had moved back to Anchorage.

I did manage to find enough coke in Anchorage to satisfy my need, but the supply did not last long. Then, the craving set in again. I felt so ashamed that I spent $600 on Christmas presents for the kids. However, the night before we were to return to Kotzebue, I blew the rest of my money, about $120, getting high. It was not enough to satisfy my yearning for the pleasure of the drug.

That vacation set the pattern for the next several trips to Anchorage. I knew I could find coke there. Between vacations,

I was able to stay clean for nine months one time, six months another. Nevertheless, my compulsion to use eventually made a mockery of my will not to use in Kotzebue.

Although I continued to do everything I'd learned in treatment and in the twelve-step meetings to stay sober, none of it seemed to have an effect on my cocaine use. I even got a new twelve-step sponsor to replace the one I'd had in Anchorage, who had grown weary of me calling only *after* I'd gotten high—never before.

I started a twelve-step meeting for drugs in Kotzebue and attended every meeting. I got high. I tried calling recovering addicts and recovering alcoholics every day. I got high. I tried calling my twelve-step sponsor frequently. I got high. I worked the twelve steps through several times. I got high. I tried going to ninety twelve-step meetings in ninety days. I got high twice.

I felt as if I were being dragged over the edge of a cliff by some unstoppable force into a future filled with pain and loneliness. Visions of devils having their way with me for eternity in glowing red dimness intruded on my imagination. When I looked to see what was dragging me down, I saw that it was me.

My pattern of relapse degenerated until the spring of 1999, when I was using once or twice a month. Perhaps that doesn't sound like much until you consider that I spent anywhere from $300 to $750 for an evening of intense smoking. I paid my bills and bought food, but that was about it. The rest of my money ended up paying for the dealers' food, bills, and new toys.

The way I smoked was very dangerous. In my quest for the perfect hit, I had developed ways to get more coke into my brain ever more quickly, using different techniques to heat the drug and control my breathing, because that is what creates the rush of pleasure. There were times when my heart pounded so hard and fast, up to 240 beats per minute, that I thought I was about to die. Instead of backing off the pipe and trying to live, I'd hit the pipe even harder and faster to get that last good hit before entering the afterlife!

"I've found that the threat of death doesn't scare someone who isn't interested in life in the first place," I later told a friend.

After the last relapse that spring, one day I found myself standing in the storm shed of my house smoking a cigarette, soaking in the implications of my latest misadventure with the drug. I smoked my cigarette outside because I don't smoke cigarettes in the house, even though I had been smoking crack inside all night long. I realized how irrational this was.

I had traded my new $1,500 hunting rifle for perhaps $225 worth of coke the night before to pay for my little pity party. That rifle was an exact replacement for another one I had traded for drugs the year before. Replacing that original rifle had been almost a moral imperative for me because I had wanted that exact rifle ever since I had seen a picture of one when I was fifteen. The rifle symbolized some of the important things I stood to gain by staying sober. Now it was gone—smoked.

As I stood there in emotional agony and abject shame, suddenly the future opened to my inner vision. I saw myself standing there on that very spot, over and over again. I saw myself without a job, my children gone, and desperately scraping money together every day to get my fix, unable to think of anything else.

I finally understood clearly that the situation never would change. It would continue to deteriorate until I had nothing, inside or out.

At that same moment, my past appeared, as if its images had been pictures painted on an enormous glass wall in the darkness; someone turned on the light behind it. I beheld, in one gestalt image, the winding, tortured path that had led me to that moment.

More than that, though, I felt I was face to face with the terror of certain death once more. Again, my Higher Power handed me The Choice.

"How badly do you want to live?" The Choice asked of me. "Are you through torturing yourself?"

I was afraid to make the choice for life, as I had thought for sure I had made that choice after every time I had gotten high since leaving treatment nearly six years earlier. All my most deliberate efforts, all my most desperate prayers, and all my brokenhearted tears had served only to bring me to my knees, staring out over the edge of a chasm filled with insane beings that delighted in giving pain. I feared that, no matter what choice I made, I would continue on to inescapable, painful death.

"Oh, God, help me!" The silent prayer seemed to tear itself from me violently.

My body walked inside to the phone; when someone answered, my voice asked for help.

I don't recall making a conscious decision to call anyone. I finally had arrived at the place where the only thing I could do to survive was to give up the struggle and surrender to the addiction. It was my Higher Power controlling my body for those few seconds. I called the hospital and asked for a counselor who had told me that she would help me when I needed it.

"I got high again last night. I can't do it any more; I need help," I told her.

"Are you ready to go back to treatment?" she asked me.

"I'm ready to do whatever it takes, as long as I don't have to use again," I said. "My life's never gonna change. It's just gonna keep getting worse until I lose everything and die. I don't want that."

"Is there someone you can call at the treatment program?"

"Yeah, there is a counselor there I've known for a few years," I told her. "I'm sure she'll be able to help me get into treatment."

After we hung up, I went to the treatment center. The counselor was at the beach on a picnic with her clients, so I left a note.

At about ten o'clock that night, with the sun still shining low across the sound, she called and then came to my home.

"Are you going to be alright for tonight?" she asked after I had told her what had been happening.

"I'll make it to work tomorrow," I said.

"What will you do if your friends come to your door with cocaine?"

"Tell them to get the heck out."

"Are you sure?"

"...I see your point."

I had to admit I had no control over whether I used. She persuaded me to check into detox that night and set up an appointment with her for an intake assessment the following morning. I was supposed to report to work that morning, but staying sober was more important.

At the intake assessment, I answered the questions truthfully the first time. I revealed everything about my history of drug use, my early childhood, my family, and how I had ended up there.

"So, am I sick?" I asked the counselor, knowing the answer.

"Oh, you're one sick puppy!" she replied.

The treatment coordinator recommended six weeks inpatient treatment, followed by two in outpatient. I agreed to the plan.

In the new program, a completely new dimension of my disease revealed itself. I finally understood that my disease had nothing to do with drug use; instead, it stemmed from an inability to react appropriately to emotional pain.

One thing I learned was that I did not know how to identify the feelings I experienced in everyday life. That became apparent whenever a counselor asked me how I felt about a given event or topic. What came out of my mouth was what I *thought* about it, not what I felt.

My counselors and I came up with a way for me consciously to know what I was feeling. I was to identify and write down three feelings every day. At first, that was surprisingly hard. I had removed myself so far from my feeling life, in an unconscious effort to keep myself from pain, that I could not say whether I was feeling joy, shame, shyness, envy, or any other feelings. I could tell only whether I felt good or bad.

The simple ability to identify my feelings was a minor revelation. I made a list of seventy-four feelings compiled from posters at the treatment center, the hospital social services office, and other feelings I identified on my own; I carried that list in my daily organizer. There were times when I could identify fifteen to twenty feelings all happening at once, such as being exhausted, confused, guilty, angry, frustrated, sad, depressed, overwhelmed, hopeful, bored, lusty, adrift, determined, innocent, loved, compassionate, and thoughtful.

Armed with the knowledge of what I was feeling at any given moment, I then could identify what was causing me to feel that way. More often than not, it was a mistaken belief about my relationships with people or with my Higher Power.

I realized one day, with a great sense of wonder at the strange twists and turns the human mind can subject itself to, that the reason I never could pick up the phone to ask for help when I was about to get high was because I did not believe that I deserved recovery. I had been struggling for years to work the twelve-step program, all the while subconsciously sabotaging my efforts. Whenever I started to feel good about whom I was and the direction my life was going, my old thought habits came out to play.

"Happiness is for other people," my thought habits told me. "I guess I'm here on Earth to be some sort of whipping boy for God. Every time things start to go my way, I can't stop myself from getting high and ruining it."

I decided I had suffered enough at my own hands. I had purchased my right to happiness and recovery with my suffering and loneliness. I now resolved that my willingness to go to any length to stay sober was the coin of the realm.

My primary counselor suggested that shame had developed into my overriding emotion. He gave me a book titled *Letting Go of Shame: Understanding How Shame Affects Your Life* by Ronald Potter-Effron and Patricia Potter-Effron, published in 1989.

From that book, I gained insights into feelings, emotions, and behaviors that shook my inner world. Aftershocks rocked me almost daily as I continued to read and communicate my findings with my counselors. Blurry understanding and more important, diffuse emotions suddenly became finely focused as I put on my new glasses.

With sharp focus, though, came sharp pain. I learned that the feelings of worthlessness and emptiness that had pervaded my entire life largely originated in a single event. The event occurred when I was five, the day I was violently exposed before a room full of people. The adult's action translated into the belief that I was a shameful creature, not worthy of existence.

I knew I had to come to terms with that event before I could deal effectively with other issues. In any case, I take full responsibility for my actions in life because I had rejected many opportunities to accept help to stop drinking and using.

Consequently, I traveled through life proving to myself that I was indeed a shameful human being, piling shame upon shame, especially after discovering alcohol. I realized I had been denied the normal progressions in life that most people take for granted, such as dating, a healthy childhood, adolescence, and adulthood— all contributing to a basic acceptance of the self. I was left to feel like some cosmic mistake. No matter what I did or where I went, I did not feel I *belonged*.

Later, I found that the sense of loss hurt terribly. I had spent my life hating who I was, while trying desperately to take care of the needs of everyone around me in an effort to show myself what they already knew: that I was a person of value. I never will be able get those years back, in part because one man decided to give the horrid gift of his own shame to a five-year-old boy.

However, I understood that it does not further my goals in recovery to cling to the resentments of old hurts. If I stayed stuck there, it would make me so uncomfortable that I would have to get high, which, in the end, would send me to prison, a mental-health institution, or the morgue. I had to make peace with my past.

I could do nothing to change my past; I had to start from where I was in life to build a true sense of self-worth. I had only vague clues as to what this mythical and wondrous state of being might look like.

"The shame does not really belong to you. It was given to you; you need to give it back to him," one counselor told me. "Perhaps you could symbolically give it back somehow, in a way unique to you."

"I'm gonna go to Sisualik, pick a bouquet of stinkweed and dead grass, and put it on his grave," I told her.

A combination of circumstances prevented me from doing that during the summer and fall. When I realized I was not going to be able to carry out my plan, I became angry and frustrated at not being able to bring closure to the issue.

"To hell with his grave, and to hell with him!" I blurted out to a friend.

Saying that brought a sudden release in my mind. It was

as if a sticky fog around me had been dispelled by a gust of cool wind. A feeling of peace and acceptance of that long-ago event settled home.

With profound feelings of discovery and regret, I found that my behaviors *were* forgivable. I discovered, upon reflection, that I already had been forgiven for most hurtful things I had done to other people.

"What would you say to someone who came to you with your story?" my primary counselor asked me one day.

"I would tell them that they needed to forgive themselves too," I replied.

When the last syllable left my mouth, I realized that briefly I had been outside myself, looking at my situation through the eyes of my counselor. After that, whenever I remembered anything that caused me to feel ashamed, I said a prayer to my Higher Power asking absolution. That was a roundabout way to achieve my aim; my Higher Power's forgiveness and my own, I understood, occurred simultaneously. In that way, I began the slow process of accepting my past the way it is—and therefore accepting myself the way I am.

I completed my treatment program in forty-eight days. I was impatient to leave. Properly run treatment programs are no fun. They are like mirrors. What I saw in the mirror was a scared little boy, always on guard against discovery. Whenever someone got close, he pulled out any number of tricks, such as turning the attention from others back on themselves. Those mental tricks were actually shields, learned through a life of running and hiding, for evading detection. I gently sat the little boy on my lap and told him he didn't have to run anymore. He was home.

My daughters had spent that spring and early summer, while I was in treatment, with my mother at Point Lay, a small Iñupiaq village. My daughters moved back into my house in Kotzebue, however, about three weeks before I got out of treatment. We were reunited, again. They were old enough this time to understand why I had to be away.

"Welcome home, Dad!" they yelled as they hugged me.

I believe that my daughters understood, in ways that no child should ever have to, that I was back home in more than one way.

This time, I had made up my mind to make the twelve-step program work. The first thing I did was attend a meeting every day, intending to make ninety meetings in ninety days. I didn't quite make all ninety meetings, but I did make it to one every time there wasn't a good reason I couldn't, or about eighty meetings. Planning every day around making a meeting keeps people in early recovery on their toes, so to speak.

I started working the twelve steps with my sponsor all over again. I did step four, making "a fearless and searching moral inventory of ourselves," as it was meant to be done. All of the fourth steps I had done before were inventories of my *behaviors*, not of the flawed morality that had caused the behaviors. I outlined the reasons I did hurtful things, thus enabling me to be rid of those earliest acquired character defects.

Later, after grappling with these issues, I started seeing a woman. I felt ready. Since I had quit drinking, I had made sufficient progress in my personal and social life. The area of love relationships was one of the last major areas I needed to develop to gain a sense of wholeness as a human being.

Like the musician, she revealed the qualities I look for in a mate. But she was unique in my experience; she was not an alcoholic, nor an addict.

"I hope you know what you're doing, getting involved with an addict," I told her.

"I've considered the possible consequences, and I know there may be problems, but you are worth it to me," she replied.

I knew that entering into an intimate relationship would bring to light any misunderstandings and immature behaviors on my part. I was right. It wasn't long before there came a time when we couldn't see each other for a week. That made me uncomfortable because I couldn't be there to observe and try to direct her thinking and behavior toward me and away from other males. I became so uncomfortable that I found that I could not live that way. I made up my mind to trust her and take her at her word. When I did that, a weight lifted from me, and I could function normally again. I found myself much more relaxed and happy with life in general.

I am grateful for the kindness, patience, and assistance I've received from my sober mentors and counselors.

I am delighted, too, to be reunited with my Higher Power, without whom it is not possible for me to stay sober and to recover. Recovery is not merely staying dry; it is not anything you *do*. That comes later. Recovery starts as a feeling from deep within. That place is hellish for the addict, a dark place of ignorance, pain, and separation. Yet I have discovered that almost all seekers of truth and peace must go to that place and shed themselves of all ulterior motives for the journey home to begin.

My feelings of hatred toward my past and myself are greatly diminished with the sweeping change of heart that occurred in my storm shed that spring morning. I still struggle occasionally with feelings of frustration, depression, and a driving need to get high, but I no longer bear them alone.

Now when I awake in the morning, I allow extra time before I get my kids up to read something about living sober and to meditate. I find this quiet time necessary to start my day on strong footing and to face whatever problems may come up. Then at the end of the day, I thank my Higher Power for helping me make it through the day without deciding to get high. The next morning, I start the process over again.

No one has guaranteed that I will live the rest of my life straight and sober. I've found that I cannot afford to live in the future any more than I can live in the past. To do so is to waste whatever today offers, which may prove a joyous occasion or a difficult lesson. Each day keeps me on the go, and sometimes it takes everything at my disposal to make my way to bed sober. I may get high tomorrow; I choose not to waste today worrying over that possibility.

When my old ways come knocking at the door of my mind, I am still just as helpless in their face as I ever was. My strength no longer lies in myself alone, though, if it ever did. My strength lies in numbers. Most important, my strength rests with whatever willingness I have on any given day to seek spiritual principles and follow the bidding of my Higher Power, whom I call Love. It is not the will of Love that I die drunk. Neither is it mine.

The boy has come home.

Afterword

Several years have passed since I finished this story. I have married a wonderful woman. We have had many lively discussions concerning the nature of addiction and its ramifications for those closest to the addict, namely me. We both have grown in understanding for what it takes for me to stay sober, and what it takes a family to remain sane through the insane times that come often in early recovery. I thank my wife with all my heart for having the courage and tenacity to stay with me through those crazy times. No woman I ever met has turned out to be the true friend that she is. I also dedicate this story to my daughters, who know more about addiction and recovery than any child should have to.

BURTON WILLIAM SILIAMII HAVILAND JR., born in 1963, is an Iñupiaq from Kotzebue. He is married and is the father of two girls. Burt worked for many years as the media coordinator for Maniilaq Association, the nonprofit social service agency of northwest Alaska. Of rural Alaska, he says, "It is difficult and slow for the worst parts of western culture to reach and take hold here."

Alaska's coastal Eskimos have hunted seals for thousands of years.

＊

GROWING UP IN RURAL ALASKA

COMPARED TO URBAN LIFE, a simpler lifestyle still prevails in rural Alaska. For many, it represents "a great place to raise kids" and a place where people are known to "look out for one another." Even time seems to move forward more slowly in rural Alaska, far away from crowds, heavy traffic, and shopping malls.

In this section, readers get a glimpse of an unusual world. Amy Reisland-Speer writes about the changes in her life she witnessed as tourism grows around Denali National Park and Preserve, while Gina M. Pope in southwestern Alaska describes the struggles and joys of her family life growing up. We travel with Burt Haviland Jr. as he recalls his education as a young Native hunter and his inward journey into manhood. Joli Morgan came to Alaska as a VISTA (Volunteers in Service to America) volunteer, married a Yup'ik woman, and taught for the University of Alaska for many years in Bethel.

Many Alaskans have made their home here after living somewhere else, including Sonja Whitethorn, who accompanied an adventurous spouse north to Alaska. Lucy Daniels examines the dramatically different life she's lived compared to her mother, who has known only village life. China Kantner, an eleven-year-old writer growing up in rural Alaska, shares a thrilling bear tale from her family's remote camp along the Kobuk River.

This section reveals how rural Alaska offers residents diverse ways of growing up.

Grizzly Bear Campground is near Denali National Park
and Preserve near Mount McKinley, above.

9

* * * * * * * * * * * *

~ DENALI NATIONAL PARK ~

Witness to changes at Denali
Amy Reisland-Speer

"**BUT DAD, YOU CAN'T BUILD** the new cabin on top of Magic Fairyland," I cried as we surveyed areas on our property many summers ago to build another cabin for our family-owned business. I had spent every summer on this land, and I considered every square inch of it to be sacred.

In 1958, before statehood, my parents had staked out fifty acres on the McKinley Park extension road at Mile 231.1 on the George Parks Highway. Back then, citizens could claim under the federal Homestead Act a trade and manufacturing site. They were required to submit to the Bureau of Land Management a plan to build businesses and show use and development of the land. The intent was to develop the area in hopes of attracting tourists and generating economic development.

The tourism-oriented business my parents chose to develop was a campground with rental cabins. We also operated a gift shop, grocery store, and liquor store between Memorial Day and Labor Day. The Denali Grizzly Bear Campground was the first and only private campground within fifteen miles of the park's entrance for some twenty years. Although the park is open year-round, most businesses close during each winter.

Denali National Park is the most popular visitor destination in Alaska, having grown dramatically since 1970 when 12,000 tourists rode shuttle buses into the park. By 2006, Denali was seeing nearly 400,000 visitors each year, according to the National

Amy Reisland-Speer at Grizzly Bear Campground near Denali in 2000

Park Service.

Long before the George Parks Highway was built, our typical family excursion to the property involved a two-day drive south from Fairbanks on the Richardson Highway, then west across the Denali Highway. Dad would try to keep us kids entertained by playing games based on spotting animals and getting points for it. I still laugh when I think of the time Dad claimed one-hundred points for spotting a dead mosquito on the windshield. If time was limited, we would travel to our property on the Alaska Railroad, getting off at Healy. Mom would scrub our faces until our skin glowed and dress us in our nicest outfits for our journey to this special place we had dubbed the "Grizzly Bear." The train was a special treat because we were allowed to pick out new coloring books, crayons, and Barbie dolls to keep us occupied for the long ride.

Television and radio signals in those days did not reach this part of Alaska. Only five families lived within a twenty-mile stretch of the gravel road. Luckily, I had a creative older brother,

Scotty, and sister, Krissi, with whom I would run free while our dog, Lovey, would bark loudly and ward off wild animals.

Dad nailed orange metal arrows to trees so we could find our way home if we strayed too far from the cabin nestled in the spruce trees overlooking the Nenana River. The train would wind by on the hillside twice daily, bringing us running to the picnic table where we would jump up and down, frantically waving our red jackets as the conductor would sound the horn year after year.

As summers went by, we began to name rocks, trees, and berry patches. Magic Fairyland and Blueberry Hill were our favorite play areas. We had defended Magic Fairyland from the "ogres" more than once. My brother would make up treasure hunts for Krissi and me by writing magic notes in cryptic script on sheets of birch bark, hiding them in special places where Krissi and I would seek them out and follow the instructions, leading us to yet another magic place or perhaps to a handful of mixed berries or vanilla-soaked toothpicks wrapped in bluebell leaves. Most mornings we would rise, leaping on our tiptoes across the cold cement floor and dashing out the door to bound across the tundra, eager to pick a cupful of blueberries for morning pancakes.

Today, the best blueberry patches have been overrun by campsites. A cabin sits where Magic Fairyland once reigned. We haven't had to fend off an ogre in ages. The guiding arrows don't direct small children home because tourists have trampled trails that run like dark scars across the tundra.

When I need time to myself, I head for my secret spot, but often someone else is relaxing there after a long day in Denali Park. Sometimes I feel infringed upon when I see our guests occupying the places where we once played and see cigarette butts littering our natural playgrounds. I

It is difficult letting go of the rocks, the trees, our sacred grounds, but along with the rest of the family, I have accepted the responsibility to cater to tourists.

have learned to block out the emotions of jealousy because these "invaders" of my land are our guests and our livelihood. We built the business to accommodate them, not ourselves, as my parents agreed when they claimed the land in the first place.

It is difficult letting go of the rocks, the trees, our sacred grounds, but along with the rest of the family, I have accepted the responsibility to cater to tourists. We provide a service, and our land provides happy memories for them as it has for us. Some mornings while at work in the office, I can hear Dad pounding nails and constructing a new cabin for the next season. Many times I have noticed the contrast of three small blond heads against the vivid tundra and mistake them for little Scotty, Krissi, and Amy.

Then, I realize they are tourist children picking berries for their morning pancakes as we once did long ago, when we were alone at the Grizzly Bear.

AMY S. REISLAND-SPEER, born in 1966, was given the nickname "Sitsoo" in the Koyukon Athabascan language. Raised in Tanana in the Interior, she lives in Healy, just outside Denali National Park. She is raising her son with her husband, Roger Speer. She is a painter in oil and egg tempera as well as owner and manager of Denali Grizzly Bear Cabins and Campground. She holds a bachelor of arts degree. The best thing about living in rural Alaska, she says, is the "closeness of community—depending on one another during times of joy and sadness."

Gina Pope at Picnic Beach near Pope-Vannoy

10

* * * * * * * * * *

~ KOKHANOK ~

Growing up at Pope-Vannoy Landing
Gina M. Pope

MY LIFE BEGAN on a small fishing boat on the Fourth of July, according to my Yukon-born mother. My father, who'd originally come to Alaska from Ohio, was not married to her. At the time, he already had a wife and six children. His homestead was in the Lake Iliamna area of southwestern Alaska, where the Aleutian Chain joins the mainland. My mother had traveled there up the Kvichak River in my dad's fishing boat, but she refused to step onto shore until my dad's first wife climbed into the mail plane and left. My dad's first wife died of hypothermia the following winter in Anchorage near Ship Creek. My mother, already pregnant with my younger sister Roberta, married my father in 1966.

Disliking the isolation and weary toil of caring for eight children, our mother left us for good. After her departure, we often had to survive on our own.

When Roberta and I were young, our mother treated us differently than the six other children left in her care. I am sure this added to the resentment my two older half-brothers, Tom and Gene Jr., felt toward us. They must have associated our arrival with their separation from their own mother.

Not liking the isolation and weary toil of caring for eight children, my mother soon left our home for good. Marlene, my half-sister, took Roberta and I for a walk along the beach on the day Mom took off for Anchorage. I remember watching the high spray of water as the mail plane lifted off the lake. Although I did not know Mom was leaving, I sensed an unusual feeling of loss.

After my mother's departure, the eight of us often had to survive on our own, which sometimes took some unusual turns. On Gene Junior's fourteenth birthday, for example, our older sister Sharon decided to make him a cake from a recipe book, but she needed eggs. "We can use seagull eggs," Tom said, and we dragged a fourteen-foot aluminum boat up a shallow, mussel-filled creek to Char Lake. In the middle of this lake sat a rocky island with numerous herring gull and arctic tern nests. We oared out to the island and collected enough eggs to make a cake.

Later that day, as I stood watching Sharon beat the whites to make frosting, my mouth watered as I thought about how good it would taste. She had my older brothers take turns beating too, since we only had a manual eggbeater. I was amazed that egg whites could beat up into a solid form! I do not remember getting a piece of cake, although I do remember my older brothers eating more than one piece each.

Another time, when Gene Junior was about twelve, he learned how to make home brew. After drinking it, he jumped into the creek out in front of our house when there was still ice on the lake and began yelling and splashing around. Tom had to pull him out of the water and scolded him for drinking "green beer," which is home brew less than seven days old. Countless other times I saw both of them drink home brew before it completely fermented, and to this day I can remember the basic ingredients—sugar, water, potatoes from the garden, oatmeal, and raisins.

Each fall, my older brothers and sisters went to stay with a boarding family in Palmer to attend school. Roberta and I were left behind with our grandparents for the winter. Grandma Pope taught us correspondence courses up to the sixth grade.

One fall, I remember standing in Grandma's turnip patch, crying when I heard the plane take off with my older half-brothers and sisters. The radishes and turnips had yellow and white flowers, and Roberta and I caught bumblebees in baby food jars.

We began to talk about our feelings. We wished Marlene would stay. It was hard to think of her being gone. For most of the summer, we would be within shouting distance of her—if not right beside her. We realized that Marlene was like our replacement mother.

What followed was a peaceful winter with our grandparents and our father. Uncle Grant Vannoy, my grandmother's brother, had a large collection of books, which I loved to browse through after school unless I was out exploring in the woods with Roberta. During the wintertime, I was content to be alive, and each spring I watched the airplane bring back Dolores, Sharon, Billy, Tom, Gene Junior, and Marlene. Often Marlene would take us on long scenic walks behind Copper Mountain or swimming at Mink Creek. We would chase baby ducklings, gather pretty rocks, and wade barefoot in the streams. The part of life that as a child I thought never would end soon would change forever.

In December 1976, our oldest brother, Bill, was lost in a blizzard while walking from Kokhanok to Pope-Vannoy. Six years later, Tom and Gene Junior capsized in large waves while crossing Lake Iliamna in a skiff. We never found their bodies. Dolores, our oldest sister, died of hypothermia after falling overboard one and a half miles from Pope-Vannoy in late October of 1985. She is buried across the creek from our grandparents' house, along with Great Uncle Grant.

My dad married a third time, having four more children. My birth mother still lives in Anchorage, and she is a wonderful grandmother to my five children. Sometimes, I wonder what life would be like if Bill, Tom, Gene Junior, and Dolores were yet alive.

Childhood is an important part of life. Perhaps my somewhat negative perception of my own childhood affected my choice of employment. I am a child advocate.

I work as a home visitor for the Healthy Families Program under the supervision of the Bristol Bay Native Association. My goal is to help prevent child abuse, but I also want to teach, as Grandma Pope did. In December 1997, I received a bachelor of arts degree in elementary education. I live, study, and work in Kokhanok, an Aleut village only fifteen miles from my childhood home.

My husband, Walter, and I often travel by boat or snowmachine to "Popes," as we now call it, packing what we need to last a week just in case we get stuck there. In the summer, the winds on Lake Iliamna must be blowing less than fifteen knots in order to cross Kokhanok Bay safely in a skiff. In the winter, the ice must be at least twelve inches thick to support all-terrain vehicles or snowmachines. The fall is the best time to cross. We arrive in a seventeen-foot skiff with a ninety-horsepower outboard when the water in the lake is at the highest level in the yearly cycle, making the probability of dinging the shaft, or lower unit, less likely. This is similar to the traveling conditions the day I arrived at Pope-Vannoy as an infant in 1965. However, I arrived in my mother's stomach after the salmon-fishing season on a twenty-four-foot fishing boat.

My grandmother and grandfather, who continued to live at Pope-Vannoy Landing, into their eighties and nineties, sometimes would reminisce with me about days gone by. Once Grandpa told me about the time Gene Junior wanted to borrow a shovel so he could make a garden. Grandpa began describing how hard it was to get people to return things they had borrowed. His rendition sounded just like the lectures he gave to us as children many years ago! I found comfort in realizing that my grandpa's recollections of the way things used to be at Pope-Vannoy were as sharp and as real as my own memories, and that I was a "good little girl," despite my troubles. (I always returned what I borrowed.)

Chief Seattle once said, "All things are connected like the blood that unites us. We did not weave the web of life; we are merely a strand in it. Whatever we do to the web, we do to ourselves."

My distressed childhood may have been the result of events that occurred shortly before I was born, yet I now have the power to influence other families' lives in a positive way.

GINA MARIE POPE, born in 1965, leads a mobile life of traveling for work within the Bristol Bay region. She enjoys berry-picking, basket-weaving, and preserving local food in Dillingham. She is a knitter for the Oomingmak Musk Ox Producers Cooperative. A state-certified teacher, Gina holds a master of education degree in early childhood. She works as an early-intervention teacher for the Bristol Bay Area Health Corporation's Infant Learning Program. In addition, she travels to villages in rural Alaska certifying candidates for associate degrees in child development for the Council for Professional Recognition, a national accreditation agency. She holds a calling in the Church of Jesus Christ of Latter Day Saints as a teacher of children in primary grades. Her personal goals include earning a doctorate to address issues of regional sustainability and being a "good person that the younger generation can love and remember."

The writer's late grandfather's house (foreground)
on Front Street in Kotzebue

11

. . . .

~ KOTZEBUE ~

A lifetime of learning
Burton W. Haviland Jr.

My Iñupiaq name is Siliamii. I was born in Kotzebue on July 6, 1963, the eldest of five siblings. Kotzebue serves as the primary staging area for hunters and seasonal campers from Kotzebue and villages along the nearby Kobuk and Noatak rivers.

My father, Burton Haviland Sr., came to Kotzebue as a young man after serving as a sonar man on a navy submarine, the USS *Tunny*. Though born in Seattle, my father as a boy had lived in Anchorage, where he attended elementary school. My mother, Lydia Haviland, was born on the banks of the Noatak River a few miles north of Kotzebue. Mom attended Mt. Edgecumbe, a boarding high school in Sitka before returning home to Kotzebue, where my parents met in the early 1960s.

Until I turned six or so, my family lived with my maternal grandfather in his small home on Shore Avenue, also known officially as "Front Street." As one might expect, Front Street follows the beach along the shore of Kotzebue Sound. When I was growing up, my extended family didn't enjoy many modern amenities such as running water and sewer, but my grandfather's home, nevertheless, enjoyed a rich Eskimo cultural tradition.

A carpenter by trade, *Ataata* (Iñupiaq for grandfather) Leslie in 1958 built his own house, a modest place measuring eighteen by twenty-five feet, including one main room in the front with windows looking out on the beach and across Kotzebue Sound, which provided a convenient way to monitor the sea or ice conditions. Leslie and the other adults frequently watched for people arriving or leaving across the shore. My grandfather also had built two small bedrooms at the back of the house. He later built a small woodshop onto the back of it, increasing the length of the house to thirty-six feet.

As his primary source of income, *Ataata* Leslie built sleds in winter and boats in the spring. His products were sought after for their high standards of craftsmanship and quality. His sleds and boats seemed to exude sleekness and speed to my little-boy eyes and smelled of wood, linseed oil, and fiberglass resin.

I remember many fall and winter days watching my grandfather in his shop, where he steamed strips of hardwood in a homemade steamer made of a five-gallon steel gas can, the sweet smell of hot, moist oak or hickory wafting through the shop. After a few hours, the strips would grow soft. Then, he would deftly bend and clamp them around frames to dry and harden for use in the various parts of basket sleds. Most of the sleds that he built were for use with snowmachines and thus were more heavily constructed than the ones designed for use with dogs.

Ataata Leslie's sleds and boats, admired for their craftsmanship and quality, exuded sleekness and speed to my little-boy eyes and smelled of wood, linseed oil, and fiberglass resin.

That little area of the beach in front of Ataata Leslie's house was the point of seemingly constant departures and returns of relatives going back and forth to camps and villages scattered across the region. More often than not, bird, seal, or caribou carcasses, representing so many of our traditional staples, graced their boats when they lighted onto shore. The carcasses smelled of blood and fat, but we all knew how delicious they would taste when cooked.

Amid this childhood backdrop, my parents and maternal relatives taught me, from my earliest childhood years, how to hunt, and also how to respect nature, including its animals, its plants, its land, its water, and most especially, the arctic weather.

In one of my earliest recollections, I remember plodding with my parents through the tundra behind Cape Krusenstern, also known locally as Sealing Point, twenty-five miles northwest of Kotzebue. Sealing Point is a traditional camping and spring hunting ground of my Iñupiaq ancestry. On that outing, I recall a high, lucent sun seeming to smile its warmth to us. A cool, gentle breeze floating in from the Chukchi Sea was constraining the mosquitoes near the tussocks that cover the earth and away from our exposed hands and faces. The cries of hundreds of birds going about their feathery errands reached us only quietly from afar. My father was carrying a shotgun; I was toting a new BB gun that Dad had given me for my recent third birthday.

"Look over there," my dad said, pointing.

In the distance, we spotted a flock of snow geese milling and waddling about in a small lake. The snow goose, a large, white, migratory bird, nests in great multitudes at Sealing Point. They were bigger than both my BB gun and me, but I decided I was going to hunt one anyway, not knowing that my gun couldn't possibly kill a goose. I immediately stopped and cocked my gun in preparation for the kill.

"Why did you cock your gun?" my dad asked.

"To shoot the ducks," I said. After all, I was a hunter now, with my shiny new gun.

"We're not close enough to them yet. You can't carry your gun ready to shoot, because you might shoot someone," Dad explained.

He solemnly took my gun from me and discharged it into the tundra with a muffled pop, then handed it back to me. Luckily for the geese, they detected our approach long before we were within range, and flapped away as we neared. I thought that at least one of them would have felt the deadly sting of my new weapon, but so went my earliest lesson in hunting—not only about safety, but also about how sensitive birds are to approaching predators, humans included.

My father taught his children much about survival on both the tundra and the sea, but the Iñupiat also hold to an enduring tradition that as part of his duty to a sister, an uncle teaches his nephews to hunt. My uncle Frank Williams—a tall, intelligent, handsome man—did not exactly teach me the oldest, most traditional, hunting and other survival practices. In this the age of the firearm, the Eskimo theory and practice of hunting with rifles was already a few generations old when I was a small child. Uncle Frank loved to hunt and teach young Iñupiaq boys to be successful hunters.

"You should try to shoot seals that are on the ice in the neck if you can," explained Uncle Frank as we approached our traditional hunting area. "That way they won't go down their breathing hole."

I was fifteen when he told me that. We were on a seal-hunting trip, negotiating his boat through the pack ice a few miles out from Sealing Point. It was springtime in early June. The days were stretching longer and longer toward the midnight sun of summer and melting away the last snows of winter. I had my first high-powered rifle, a 7mm magnum. I figured this rifle would dispatch seals of any size so suddenly that they wouldn't ever move after being hit. In fact, I thought it ridiculous to restrict myself to only one spot on a seal to shoot for. It was my opinion that the adult hunters used rifles that were underpowered. I was about to learn—painfully—that the raw power of a rifle could be irrelevant.

As we tooled around in the pack ice, we spied a huge *ugruk*, or bearded seal, sleeping on a little iceberg about 150 yards from the edge of the ice. As we approached the iceberg as slowly and as quietly as our outboard motor would allow, everyone with a rifle, including my three brothers, Uncle Frank, and another uncle or two, crowded onto the bow of the boat and took aim. There must have been six or seven of us.

"Wait until it puts its head up," Frank whispered.

Because of my youth, I ignored him. I decided to shoot the animal through the shoulders. When I had the shot placement I wanted, I fired. Blooie! One of my brothers fired a second after me, though more from surprise than intent. I believe my bullet struck where I aimed it, but not where my uncle said it should go.

The ugruk arched forward and slid down its escape hole,

probably already dead, but now sinking irretrievably to the floor of the sea.

The silence that followed seemed to fill the whole world.

Everyone but Frank tried not to look at me. I held my rifle limply, looking at the bottom of the boat. Humiliated, I made my way to the back of the boat and stayed there for the rest of the trip.

I couldn't believe what had happened. I'd let my pride and ego cloud my judgment, sending a precious animal to the bottom of the sea. It would be many years before I would have a chance to redeem myself.

"Don't shoot an ugruk in the head unless it's in the water and unless you can get to it and spear it before it sinks," Uncle Frank told me during another hunt.

The reason, I learned, is simple. The arctic seal has evolved a nervous system response over tens of thousands of years that causes its body to arch downward into its escape hole when there is even the slightest hint of danger, such as an approaching polar bear or hunter. Consequently, any shot that does not disable the spinal chord will allow a seal to escape. Even a shot to the head of a seal, which is instantly fatal, will not stop its spinal chord from firing the messages that instruct its body to arch into the water.

Ever since those early learning experiences, I've believed that only a shot to the neck would incapacitate a seal with immediacy. However, after a successful seal hunt one spring, by then in my mid-thirties, I discussed the best place to shoot seals with Bob Uhl, a long-time seasonal resident of Sisualik, a subsistence camp ten miles or so across the sound from Kotzebue.

"The old-time hunters maintained that any shot to the spine, even at the place where it connects to the pelvis, would have the desired effect," Bob explained.

So, my education in hunting continues. No one person could possibly learn everything there is to know about hunting in the arctic, but I have learned not to let my ego cause the unnecessary loss of animals. As I've matured and learned more about the way seals were hunted before the advent of the rifle in this area, I've come to respect the knowledge and experience of my Iñupiaq instructors. I realize how precious the lives of animals are.

I still use a rifle, but I'm no longer so cavalier about shooting animals.

Burton William Siliamii Haviland Jr., born in 1963, is an Iñupiaq from Kotzebue. He is married and is the father of two girls. Burt worked for many years as the media coordinator for Maniilaq Association, the nonprofit social service agency of northwest Alaska. Of rural Alaska, he says, "It is difficult and slow for the worst parts of western culture to reach and take hold here." Burt looks forward to someday building new homes both in Kotzebue and at camp, where he can enjoy retirement.

Caribou hunter at sunset

12

· · · · · · · · · · · ·

~ BETHEL ~

Did you think it was a matter of life or death?

Joli Morgan

I ENVY PEOPLE WHO REMEMBER vast storehouses of paren-
tal words of wisdom. I do not have parents in the mother-father,
nuclear-family sense, for I was raised by my grandmother in
Beverly Hills while my mother was striving to be a bohemian in
San Francisco. My mother's words of wisdom were linked to her
problems trying to survive as a female artist in a society that sometimes viewed single mothers as once removed from prostitutes.

"Men are bastards" was as close as my mother got to wisdom.

So, without the words of a father or brother or sister, I found
refuge in the words of my teachers. These Christian brothers of
the Roman Catholic Church did have quantities of verbal, if narrow, wisdom. For example, "When you go to bed, wrap the rosary
around your right hand." This actually worked for me about two
out of every seven nights. Or, "It is just as sinful to think a lewd
thought as to do a lewd act." As an adolescent I was so busy thinking, I had neither the time nor the courage to act, but according to
the Christian brothers, I was a sinner just the same.

By eighth grade, I had moved with my mother to Chicago,
where my teachers were nuns who believed in applying rulers to
the back of the knuckles. Pain seemed their main motivation. Yet,
when it came time to graduate from middle school, these stern
women took me to a department store and bought me my first
suit, complete with alterations. High school returned me to the

brothers, whose words to save you from hell were spoken in Latin. I learned that Britain is an island but Europe is not. On one humid afternoon, with the classroom windows wide open, and while looking across at the girls' classroom, I learned to conjugate: amo, amas, amant.

Chicago is known as the Windy City. When the wind arrives, people say, "The hawk is out tonight." Two Chicago winters broke my mother. One night, sick, and unemployed, she told me that we were going to the then-segregated South. Soon we were riding a Greyhound bus to New Orleans. I heard my first southern words from the mouth of a Mississippi state trooper. I was sleeping on the back seat of the bus. He was tapping my shoe with his baton. I looked up. He looked down. "Son, move to the front of the bus." I moved to the front of the near-empty bus, passing one old black man, and sat next to my mother.

At a private high school in Eunice, Louisiana, the Arcadia Baptist Academy, lay teachers replaced men and women of the cloth as my educators. This boarding school came complete with a church and a baptismal pool. In the dorm after lights went out, I learned about girls and farm animals. In my civics class, our teacher slowly explained to us the difference between the North and the South in America. "In the North, Negroes are loved as a race but hated as individuals. In the South, we hate them as a race but love them as individuals." I repeated this story often until a Southerner from Alabama said, "I don't know about the 'love' part, but if it was true, it was only as long as they were doing what we wanted."

Private school proved expensive, and my mother's health was not improving, so I dropped out of high school at seventeen and joined the U.S. Navy. "Men, welcome to the United States Navy Recruit Training Center and to San Diego. I want you to remember these words: You're seaman recruits. That means you're lower than whale shit. And where's whale shit? It's at the bottom of the ocean." The navy was rich with this kind of wisdom. If it moves, salute it; if it doesn't move, paint it.

After I left the Navy in 1959, the next eight years became a virtual kaleidoscope of clichés that started with "Man…" and ended with "...later, man." Finally, I came up for air and found that I was still alive, if somewhat damaged. Some of my friends didn't make it. Robert tumbled from beer to pot to shooting methamphetamine, while Madeline, after escaping from a psychiatric ward, took more LSD and jumped out of a third-story window. Eventually I sought repentance and redemption. While attending college in Vermont in the late 1960s, the federal government reached out to me with an offer to become a Volunteer in Service to America (VISTA) in Alaska. Loaded down with cases of canned bacon and Tang, a ratty old sleeping bag, the latest Eddie Bauer parka, and a Bob Dylan album, I was deposited via float plane in Kasigluk, a Yup'ik village twenty miles west of Bethel in southwest Alaska. My VISTA partner, Chuck, and I were determined to save this tiny village from the very government that had sent us there. Our training manual stressed that "PROCESS IS MORE IMPORTANT THAN PROJECT." We were to follow a kind of western version of Taoism.

For the village itself, however, we simply provided a year of comic relief. Chuck and I immediately worked on projects: library, newsletter, Adult Basic Education, and Head Start, the normal activities that new settlers bring to the Last Frontier. If we had stayed a second year, no doubt a community theater, with the help of the local schoolteachers, would have topped our what-the-village-needs list. Of course, three months passed before we thought to ask the village what the village wanted. Not surprisingly, a newsletter was not on their list.

In the arctic, survival is a full-time occupation. For our part in Kasigluk, rather than the whole village having to spend each of 365 days worrying about what stupid mistake we would make today, we each were assigned on a rotating basis to a family, bringing casual invitations for tea, steam baths, and boating and hunting trips. After our first week, from waking to sleeping, we were never left alone.

"Did you think it was a matter of life or death?" These words of wisdom were relayed to me on a hunting trip with men from my adopted family. The Johnson River cuts across the tundra from the Yukon River and flows south into the Kuskokwim River. In the predawn, we had left the village by boat heading up the Johnson River. It was an early fall hunting trip for wild celery and spinach, moose, ducks, geese, beaver, bear, and anything else that was edible. Seven of us had crowded into two boats. We had drums of gas, tents, rifles, shotguns, dried fish, and, for Chuck and I, food in cans. We moved in and out of the sloughs, lakes, and rivers as we journeyed north. After first light, we began to stop every thirty minutes and climb the low riverbank to look across the flat, treeless tundra for game.

Rather than the whole village worrying about our stupid mistakes, we were assigned on a rotating basis to families, bringing invitations for tea, steam baths, and boating and hunting trips.

We didn't see game or any other hunters until late in the afternoon when we came across three teenage boys from the village. They were heading toward us in an old wooden boat using a thin stick as a paddle. We stopped and slid alongside their boat. The conversation was in Yup'ik, but I gathered their outboard motor had broken down. After a couple of minutes, one of the men handed one of the boys half of a pack of cigarettes. Then we left them. Above the noise of our outboard, I turned to one of the men and yelled, "Shouldn't we go back and tow them to the village?" He smiled and looked at me for a long time. "Did you think it was matter of life and death?" he asked. No one ever had asked me to judge an action by such a measure. I thought about his question. The boys were young and strong, knew their way, and had food, dry clothing, and matches. The temperature was above freezing. "No," I said. He smiled again. "Neither did we," he said.

And so, as I grew up, I gathered all these bits and pieces of wisdom in life from classmates, teachers, chief petty officers, and Yup'ik hunters. I did ask my mother once for words of wisdom. It was one of those innocent childhood questions that touch on death. I asked my mother what she would do if she were to live again. "I'd risk more," she said.

Years later, when my mother lay dying in a hospital outside of Lihue, Hawaii, she asked me to read to her a poem, "Do Not Go Gentle into that Good Night," by Dylan Thomas. The poem starts with:

> *Do not go gentle into that good night,*
> *old age should burn and rave at close of day;*
> *rage, rage against the dying of the light.*

I understood the poem, and I understood why my mother had asked me to read it that bright, searing hot day in Hawaii. This was a matter of life and death.

JOLI BRIAN MORGAN of Bethel in southwestern Alaska, who was born in 1937, did not grow up living a subsistence lifestyle. But his wife, Ina, is a Yup'ik, and he shares these activities with her. He holds a master's degree in business administration from Clarkson University in New York. A father of two boys, he came to Alaska with Volunteers in Service to America (VISTA) in 1967 and has worked as a professor and interim director at Kuskokwim Campus, a University of Alaska branch in Bethel, where he is a professor emeritus. He looks forward to spending more time at fish camp.

Jim & Sonja Whitethorn

13

. . . .

~ PETERSBURG ~

New life for a "quiet girl" from the Midwest
Sonja Whitethorn

EVEN A SHY, QUIET GIRL from a sleepy Midwestern town's class of 1966 can be coerced into adulthood in a far-from-commonplace life. She just has to marry the "right" man, one who presents his dreams and ideas so enthusiastically and confidently that you feel you are depriving yourself of a wonderful experience if you don't jump right in and lend a helping hand. Frankly speaking, no matter how it may, at times, have appeared that I *wished* for a quiet, boring life, it hasn't happened, not yet.

Being married for so many years to a Whitethorn is like riding an eighteen-wheeler at one-hundred miles an hour. I met Jim at a dance the summer before our senior year of high school. I remember wearing a black sweatshirt with black stretch pants and black Beatle boots. Jim brought me home in his brown 1954 Chevy, walked me to the door, and shook my hand. I was impressed with his ambition, sense of humor, and sensitivity. He worked on a farm, "shoveling shit" as he described it, for two dollars an hour, to earn money for his first ticket to Alaska. Jim felt guilty if he didn't work twelve-hour days.

Jim and I came from similar backgrounds. Our fathers were both postmasters who served in World War II. Our mothers stayed home and raised kids. Religion was important for both families, although Jim was Catholic, and I was Protestant.

Jim and I dated on and off for four years. Jim's dad cautioned him about getting his lip stuck in my braces. We were constantly teased about being Mutt and Jeff. Jim stands six-foot-five and I am five-foot-one if I stretch. Jim would like to have people around him twenty-four hours a day. I need alone time. Though different in stature and personality, we have made it work.

Oh, yes, while dating, Jim broke up with me many times. One lame excuse was that he couldn't come see me because he had to spend "a lot of money" on his car. At my thirty-year high school reunion, a college friend of Jim's said he never knew if we were dating or not. Often, neither did I. At one point, I spent three months in Milwaukee training in pediatrics and got "pinned" to someone else. Then Jim met me at the airport and asked me to marry him. A year later, on June 6, 1969, we did.

I graduated from nurse's training, took two days of qualifying examinations, and got married all in the same week. The next day, we left for Alaska. I spent the second night of marriage sleeping on the floor of the Seattle airport terminal sandwiched between Jim, his dad, his brother, and a cousin, all of whom would be living with us in a one-bedroom trailer for the summer. I never had seen the ocean. Therefore, landing in Sitka for the first time, where the jet meets the water as it comes to a stop, was a breath-holding experience.

I never had seen the ocean. Therefore, landing in Sitka for the first time, where the jet meets the water as it comes to a stop, was a breath-holding experience.

Honestly, I did try to tell my in-laws that I did not know how to cook. After the first week, I made them all believers. I've blocked out most of it but have lingering memories of raw meat, lime Kool-Aid, and French toast that dripped. They all tolerated my cooking silently. For my part, I put up with their genetically instilled desire to play jokes on people.

The famous purse trick is a good example of the legendary Whitethorn humor. A large purse with money pinned to the outside is placed in the middle of the street. Invisible monofilament fishing line is attached to the purse at one end and a hidden

Whitethorn at the other, who then waits for a concerned and/or greedy citizen to approach and reach for the purse. Just as the person's hand touches the purse, the fishing line is given a big jerk. I have to admit, remembering the shocked look on people's faces still makes me chuckle.

In 1970, we moved back to the Midwest for Jim's last year of college, where he became a certified teacher. With me working as a registered nurse, I envisioned us contented with nine-to-five jobs, good medical benefits, and a comfortable retirement. Life would be predictable. I like that. Change, for me, is a scary word. But not for Jim. I had married a mover and a shaker!

We returned to Petersburg, our island home in Alaska. Jim taught school for two years, and then became a building contractor so he could "take time off and go moose hunting in the fall." He also tried a laminating business, with me being second in command; he invented a patented paper-towel holder; he built, owned, and cooked in a combination restaurant and store; he tried to sell oil from the pipeline to tourists, and on and on. Jim then became a commercial fisherman, owns a storage facility and a crane, and drives pilings for home foundations built on muskeg. So, in addition to nursing, I can catch fish, pilot commercial fishing boats, shingle roofs, tape walls, trowel cement, run a winch and boom, and most important, raise children. I've been so busy I haven't had time to wonder what happened to quiet and predictable.

The kids are adults now. Jamie teaches English and coaches a debate team in Montana. Luke is a commercial fisherman like his dad.

I'm a little more assertive and a little less quiet today, although I'm still 99% sure I'd choose death over giving a speech.

Working a twelve-hour day is no longer "in" with Jim. Six months of work and six months of play is. I'm taking the time to ask myself what is important to me. My all-important "soul goal" is to become a good freelance writer. When I informed my dear husband that I had enrolled in two writing courses, his first response was "Oh, noooooooo."

Today, Jim is supporting me in my goals as I supported him in his. We both have made changes without losing who we basically are. After decades of compromise, we are at ease with each other. I've helped Jim become comfortable with comfortable. Jim has helped me become comfortable with change.

SONJA JEAN WHITETHORN, born in 1948, lives in Petersburg in southeast Alaska and spends a part of each winter in Thousand Palms, California. She has a son who fishes and a daughter who is an English teacher. A retired registered nurse and a commercial halibut fisherman, Sonja finds kinship with her grandmother who homesteaded alone near the Black Hills of South Dakota, living in a sod shanty. The best thing about rural Alaska, she says, is "the relaxed lifestyle, the willingness of people to help one another in times of need, and the awesome beauty."

The Class of 2009 gathers at Mount Edgecumbe High
School, a state-run boarding school since the late 1940s.

14

* * * * * * * * * * *

~ GOLOVIN ~

What might have been in a changing world
Lucy Nuqarrluk Daniels

AT BETHEL'S FIRST Public Health Service Hospital in September of 1946, I was born into a world that my mom, Sophie K. Coolidge, and I would share for the next seventeen years, the first eleven at Nunapitchuk and the next six in Eek, two outlying villages in the Bethel region of southwest Alaska. Though two brothers, Joseph and Charles, had preceded my entry into the Coolidge family, Charles died when I was only about a year old. At about three, I became the big sister to another brother, David, who sadly died before his first birthday.

After David came Alice, Sophia, Arthur, John, Nan (now Julie), Sally ("Polly" to us) and Mollyanne. By the time Sophia arrived, I was old enough to help wash cloth diapers, the only kind available then, by rubbing them in an up-and-down motion against the glass washboard. Standing on a chair, I also washed dishes in a metal pan on top of the round table our Dad made. After washing each dish in warm water, foamy from a pinch of Tide laundry detergent, I placed it upside down on a dish towel. At about the same time, I started trying my hand at cutting salmon for dry fish at fish camp in the summer. I helped gather greens and berries, of course. I also plucked ducks, but once when a teeny black bug scurried up my arm, I dropped a half-plucked bird and left it for someone else to finish.

Two brothers later—Art and John, who were about thirteen

months apart—and after we had moved to Eek, I skinned my first muskrat. To my embarrassment, however, its intestines oozed out through a hole I accidentally cut. After Julie—then called Nan—joined us, I graduated from the eighth grade at the local school in Eek in May 1963. Completion of the eighth grade was called "graduation," probably because it was the highest grade a village young person could attain at that time. As I filled out a lengthy, detailed application to attend Mt. Edgecumbe High School, a boarding school in Sitka, I couldn't have foreseen that Polly and Molly later would make us a family of nine children, nor could I have known the weight of the decision to leave the secure world that Mom and I had shared.

Nevertheless, in August 1963, at seventeen, I boarded a Northern Consolidated Airlines Fokker F-27 in Bethel, flying out of southwestern Alaska, to attend this school hundreds of miles away in southeast Alaska. (I was starting high school late because I had entered school late at age six and had been held back twice.) From that moment on, my life never would again resemble Mom's. Years before, when Mom was just seventeen, she already had been married for about four years and was caring for her first son, who would have been about two.

As I flew to Anchorage, a woman walked around the plane distributing pieces of chewing gum to the passengers. Until then, I only had ridden in small planes that passengers crawled into. The Anchorage International Airport terminal was the largest building I had ever seen. As I ate my first hamburger and potato chips in Anchorage, I watched my fellow travelers and, like them, placed a piece of round bread on the top and bottom of the piece of round meat.

Leaving Anchorage, I rode in a huge, quiet jet to Juneau, where we boarded another strange-looking float plane equipped with propellers, all right, but inside we had to sit sideways. As if that weren't strange enough, we splashed down into the water and taxied up onto a huge flat ramp paved with cement. When the "Goose," as the airplane was called, splashed down into the Sitka Channel, my life as a boarding-school student began, far away from my village, both geographically and culturally.

Attending high school away from my home village would determine the course of the rest of my life. Like so many other young rural Alaska Natives of that era, by choosing to attend boarding high school, I had moved unwittingly into a world that was foreign to both Mom and me. While Mom remained in the world into which she had been born, I was moving into and learning the much different ways of a foreign world known as "western culture," which I previously had glimpsed only through films, books, and the words of elementary schoolteachers.

What would my life have been like had I stayed in my traditional Yup'ik Eskimo village of 200 or so? Well, had I opted to stay home, marriage probably would have been arranged by my parents and those of my husband soon after I had "become a woman." For me, that was age fifteen. For Mom, it had been age thirteen, which is when she married Dad. After Mom had seen some of her six daughters off to boarding high schools, she told me, "I didn't know we were but girls back then when we got married." (Read: "acquired husbands.")

Had I stayed in my village, most likely I would have moved in with my husband's family, just as Mom had done after her marriage had been arranged with Dad, Calvin K. Coolidge. She told me that she moved to the tent that Dad and his mother, my grandmother, shared at fish camp after my mom's father and the rest of her family had moved back to the village without her at the end of the summer.

"I found out, then, that I had 'acquired a husband,'" she explained to me many years later.

Traditionally, a man and woman did not "get married" in the Yup'ik culture as they did in the western culture. Instead, a man acquired a wife and a woman acquired a husband. The wedding ceremony, probably introduced by the missionaries in

> Like many other young Alaska Natives, by choosing to attend a boarding high school away from my village, I moved unwittingly into a world foreign to both Mom and me.

the early 1900s, is called "the formation of a circle." Thus, when Mom moved in with Dad and his mother, they "formed a circle" in August 1939.

I had thought that a young girl moved in with her husband's family to learn how to care for her husband's catch of fish, game, and waterfowl, but Mom said she learned such things mostly on her own. She said she performed menial household tasks, such as washing dishes and tidying up, in her new home, and that she learned to sew animal skins into clothing by watching, then trying. This probably would have been my lot, had I stayed in the village. I probably would have been learning how to pluck, clean, and cut up a goose to make tasty soup.

Instead, in a home-economics class at my boarding high school for Alaska Natives, I was learning the correct way to prepare a strange kind of food called a grapefruit—first cutting it in half, then slitting it along its sections just to the rind, and finally sweetening it with sugar. It was then ready to eat with a spoon. (I later discovered that I preferred grapefruit plain.)

If I had remained in my village, I would have learned to cut and fit together muskrat or rabbit skin pieces into a warm, wind-proof parka—a marvelous art. Instead, faraway in my high school home-economics class, I was cutting out and sewing together sleeves, front and back pieces, and a collar from white fabric to make a blouse—complete with ruffles!—on a foot-operated treadle sewing machine.

When I lived at home, Mom had made most of my clothes. From the ever-handy flour and sugar sacks, she made undergarments, as well as window and cupboard covers, and dresses from store-bought fabric. Clothes were worn mainly to cover one's body and to keep it warm. In high school, however, "matching" suddenly became important. That is, no longer could I wear a floral-print blouse with a plaid skirt.

After finishing high school, I made do with winter gear from Eddie Bauer, L. L. Bean, and later, Cabela's. Because of my inability to outfit my husband and children in handcrafted parkas, hats, mitts, and boots, I thank these companies for saving me the embarrassment of having an ill-clothed family. I might have been

treated like a very nice, fun-loving Eskimo woman who was criti-
cized by the women in her village because she couldn't sew skin
parkas, hats, and boots. Unlike me, she couldn't use high-school
attendance as an excuse. I heard that the other women said of her,
"All she can do is laugh."

Although I can clean and cut a fish by using my fingers as
guides to leave an even amount of meat next to the skin, the
part we usually eat, I have yet to complete the whole fish-drying
process in the style of the Kuskokwim area—cutting, drying,
smoking—as my sister Sophia has done. As a result, I rely on my
sister's generosity to satisfy my craving for that brand of dried
fish. (Unlike the title character in "The Little Red Hen," who refused to share her freshly baked bread with her animal friends
because each one refused to help plant, reap, take to the mill,
and bake into bread a grain of wheat, my sister gladly shares the
results of her hard work with me, though I don't help out.) After
Mom put down her *uluaq* (Eskimo woman's knife)—as far as fish
cutting was concerned—Sophia ably took her place.

At the time I left the village to attend high school, the whole
village, except the teachers, spoke Eskimo. Since Mom spoke only
Eskimo, she and I conversed exclusively in this language. Before
the 1970s, we called our language *Yugcetun* (meaning "like a
person"), and we called ourselves *Yuut* (meaning, "the people").
In about 1972, our language began to be called *Yup'ik* (meaning,
"real person," in the lower Yukon Eskimo dialect) and we became
known as Yup'iks ("real people"), which is somewhat anglicized.
Had the lower Kuskokwim and Bristol Bay dialect been chosen,
we would be called "Yupiaqs" ("real people," anglicized), the plural
being *Yupiat*.

Before I left the village in which I had lived with Mom and
Dad for seventeen years, English was my second language, if a
language one speaks only to a teacher or teachers' children can
be called a second language. Even at school, my schoolmates and
I conversed in Eskimo. Whenever our teacher ordered us to speak
English, we grew mute. The teacher wanted us to converse in a language we barely knew. For instance, we couldn't have recounted a
tale in English as well as we could in Eskimo, much less converse

with each other freely and comfortably.

After starting boarding high school, English gradually became my everyday language. Although I had learned the mechanics of English, I had no real need to speak it consistently until I entered high school, where my friends from southeast Alaska and the Aleutian Islands didn't understand what later became known as Yup'ik Eskimo. Interestingly, as I began speaking more English than Eskimo in my second year, the characters who did the talking in my dreams gradually became the English-speaking people only, while those who couldn't speak English, such as my parents, only mumbled unintelligibly. When I returned to the village in the spring of 1965, I could hardly speak Eskimo at first. While Mom and my younger brothers and sisters watched, I would unpack an item from my suitcase and try to think of words to say in Eskimo. I knew what to say in English but didn't know how to translate it into Eskimo. I found myself close to tears because I missed my faraway high school so much. Fortunately, I felt better after my first day back.

By then, largely because of my choice to enter boarding high school, I lived in a world about which Mom knew very little, having lived her whole life in Yup'ik villages. However, she has not forced the old Eskimo ways on me. Instead of arranging my marriage in accordance with the traditional Yup'ik custom, she allowed me to choose my own husband, although I waited until my thirties to marry. When I was a girl, teen pregnancy, as it is defined today, rarely occurred, because young girls were married off soon after puberty. I remember a mother who expressed relief because her fifteen- or sixteen-year-old daughter had "acquired a husband" before she became pregnant. If this was Mom's fear for me, she never expressed it. What made her happy, though, was when one of her children finished schooling, be it high school or college. I recall one year, when two of my male cousins chose to get married instead of returning to high school in the fall, Mom complained. "The women kept them from continuing their education." She said this not meaning to pass ill judgment on the young women. Mom simply was expressing disappointment that the two boys had chosen marriage instead of education.

Similarly, though Mom and I live in different worlds, I don't judge Mom by my newfound knowledge and practices. For instance, in my notorious home-economics class, I learned how to set the table—the fork on the left of the plate atop a folded napkin, the table knife on the right, and the teaspoon next to the knife. When I visit Mom, though, I help myself to a plate, either from the stack of plates on the kitchen table or from the cupboard, and the silverware from a container of forks or spoons from the table or from a shelf where silverware containers are kept. We all shared one or two table knives to butter bread or Sailor Boy Pilot Bread, a staple in rural Native villages, while napkins were distributed as needed. As for table manners at Mom's, I only need to ask, "Now where's the salt?" and someone passes it to me. In my own home, I do set my table "properly," as I had learned, and am teaching my young daughter to do so as well.

From the time I started taking my breaks from boarding high school every summer, I have flown in and out of Mom's world. Although Mom and I live worlds apart, we have always been friends. Because Mom exists within the boundaries of the Yup'ik village, she never will understand fully all the complexities of my world, but I admire her for allowing me to navigate in this "other" world.

LUCY NUQARRLUK DANIELS, born in 1946, lived in Golovin, Alaska, for almost thirteen years. A Central Yup'ik, she has raised two children. Born into a family of nine children, she grew up in the lower Kuskokwim area of southwest Alaska. Her family lived a subsistence lifestyle. "Our primary food was fish, which we dried and smoked in the summer and put away for the winter," she recalls. "Today, we still depend on fish and moose for sustenance, though not to the extent we did when I was a child." Lucy earned a bachelor's degree in Yup'ik Eskimo at the University of Alaska Fairbanks and completed a secondary teaching certificate with an endorsement in history. She is currently working toward a master's degree in education. In addition, she has received training to assist victims of abuse. She and her family live in Soldotna, Alaska, on the Kenai Peninsula.

A bear makes itself at home at the Kantner camp.

15

. . . .

~ KOBUK RIVER CAMP ~

The Bear
China Kantner

AT SIX IN THE MORNING, Dad awoke to our black dog, Worf, sniffling and whining on the plywood floor of our cabin. It was springtime at my favorite place in the world: our camp along the Kobuk River in northwest Alaska. I was ten, and a heavy sleeper. My mom had returned to Kotzebue and her job. Dad and I were on our own.

Still groggy, Dad stumbled over to the window, to see what Worf was fussing about. Inside the *qanisaq* (arctic entryway), a foot from the window, sat a black bear. The bear spotted Dad and scrambled away. Then Dad turned to the brown-haired lump in bed across the room.

"Wake up, China!" said Dad. "There's a bear out here."

It took some vigorous shaking before I woke up and yawned.

"You sure it isn't Clarence?" I mumbled, reaching for my glasses.

"Yeah, I'm sure," laughed Dad, as he walked back to the window.

This was far from the first time bears have visited our camp. One day, long before I was born, Dad was alone at the cabin. He answered a knock at the door, thinking it was his good friend Clarence. Instead, Dad discovered a bear's nose pressed against the window pane. That's one of my favorite stories. Now, another bear was visiting. I got out of bed and made my way to the window.

"I can't see it," I complained, so Dad moved me to a different angle.

There in a flickering ray of sunlight stood the bear, the sun radiating off of its big black nose.

"Wow! I love bears," I said. "Is he gorgeous or what? Male, right?"

"Yep, good job, China P," Dad replied.

(Somehow that "P" attached itself to my name when I was little, so now my parents rarely use just my first name.)

Dad opened the cabin window and took out the screen. He aimed his camera at the bear and started clicking. The bear moseyed down to our little tin boat, the one we use to ferry up the tributaries of the Kobuk River near our camp. Dad and I worried our visitor might sink the little boat. Mom always jokes about that boat being made out of aluminum pop cans. I don't drink pop, but that boat sure seemed thin. The bear sniffed at some old blood left in the boat from a caribou earlier that spring. Then he placed one paw in the bow. Immediately the boat descended into the water, startling the bear. He sniffed once more before strolling onto the tundra.

A moment later, Dad and I climbed back into our beds. I lay there, thinking of all the other times bears had wandered into our camp. When I was three, a bear had come through our yard and ate all the food in our qanisaq.

The bear was standing on his hind legs, pushing on our door. Mom was pushing back, while Dad put his pants on, and got the gun. I was in bed.

"Oh, he's so cute!" I kept saying.

My dad shot the bear through the open window. Even today, fading blood stains remain on the floor of the qanisaq.

The next year, we had caribou meat hanging by the food cache. One morning, we awoke to find it had disappeared. That evening, I was standing by the chopping block, playing with kindling, when the bear that had stolen our food appeared at the woodpile. Mom snatched me up and rushed into the house.

I sat up in bed, entering the present, feeling watched. The bear was sitting outside our window.

"Dad, the bear's back," I said.

Both of us jumped out of bed. Dad grabbed his camera while I opened the window. Worf heaved himself out from under the bed. The bear sniffed the stinky pot by the old birch tree where we store scraps. He sat down and ate everything in the pot: goose wings, rotting eggs, duck feet, caribou hair. Finishing up, the bear licked his lips before walking out of sight. Hardly a moment later, we heard bear claws scratching on the roof.

The bear stood on hind legs, pushing on our door. Mom pushed back, while Dad put on his pants. "He's so cute!" I said. Then my dad fired through the open window.

I winced. "I hope he doesn't punch through the skylight!" I said.

Dad had always told me to be careful around the skylight. Amazingly, the bear managed to step around the skylight. He finally stepped off the roof to enjoy a long, leisurely drink from our water barrel. Thankfully, he didn't tip it over. My arms ached from hauling buckets of river water up the hill to the house. The bear lay down next to the pot again. He held it with his claws. He licked it out for a long time. Dad kept clicking away with his camera. After awhile I got bored.

"Hey Dad, can you hold my legs while I lean out the window and get my slingshot and some ammunition from the shelf?" I asked.

The night before I'd begged my dad to help me make a slingshot. I wanted one because he had one when he was growing up at this same camp. I'd also gone hunting for moose turds for ammunition.

"I told you that you might want your slingshot," said Dad with an I-told-you-so smile. "I'm not letting you lean out the window with a bear out there. You'd get me in trouble with your mom."

The bear finished licking out the pot and walked around to the other set of windows. I put my hand to the window. The bear leaned his head toward my hand. He hit his nose on the glass trying to reach me. He opened his mouth to try to get in. He hit his teeth on the glass, looking shocked.

"I hope you're taking pictures, because this is awesome," I whispered to Dad.

The bear turned and lumbered down the hill and out of sight out toward the tundra.

Afterward, I prepared my breakfast, wondering if I'd ever see that bear again.

CHINA QALUKISUQ KANTNER, born in 1997, is *Purely Alaska's* youngest contributor. China has grown up in northwest Alaska in the outdoors and out in the country gathering food with her family and living off the land. She and her family pick wild berries, fish in the rivers and the sea, and hunt caribou, moose, musk ox, ducks, geese, and rabbits. Just eleven when she wrote her bear tale for this anthology, China completed two college classes while in sixth grade and enjoyed the challenge. She says she likes living in rural Alaska and especially staying at her family's camp, "which is my favorite place in the world."

Caribou crosses a river.

✳

HARVESTING THE LAND AND SEA

MANY RURAL ALASKANS live close to the land. They harvest fish, game, berries, and other foods from the wild, in every season. Alaska's indigenous population has been pursuing this "subsistence" way of life since time immemorial, and today many non-Native Alaskans gather subsistence foods from the wild as well.

Native peoples of Alaska, like American Indian tribes farther south, always lived traditionally by placing the importance of the group over that of the individual in gathering food for all tribal members and sharing it with everyone who traveled in close-knit bands.

In today's modern world, many Alaskans routinely harvest wild food from the land and water, feeding themselves physically and spiritually, and more often than not taking part in the cash economy. Commercial fishing also remains a huge part of Alaska's way of life through its rural regions.

Fierce battles have raged for decades among those who take part in the sport, subsistence, and commercial fisheries as they all compete for this extraordinary, if finite, natural resource. Likewise, Alaska hunting factions find subsistence harvesters pitted against recreational hunters who fly into remote regions statewide to bag their trophy fish and game. Nevertheless, rural Alaskans cherish a way of life that nourishes their spirit from connecting their everyday lives to Alaska's land, sea, lakes, and rivers.

In this section, readers can chuckle with Sonja Whitethorn as she shares part of her life in Alaska. In "Tales from the Open Sea," she connects us through humor-laced prose with a commercial fishing trade shared by people pursuing similar livelihoods throughout the world. Steve Pilz, a long-time rural Alaska school-teacher, writes about a special fishing spot "way up" the Pah River in northwest Alaska, while Emma Snyder describes how members of her family harvest their caribou meat each fall, a centuries-old pursuit inextricably linked to her traditional Iñupiaq culture.

Historical photo of fishing fleet in Petersburg

16

∙ ∙ ∙ ∙ ∙ ∙ ∙ ∙ ∙ ∙ ∙ ∙

~ PETERSBURG ~

Tales from the open sea
Sonja Whitethorn

MY HUSBAND JIM ASKED ME to go halibut fishing in 1983 in the same tone of voice other husbands reserve for asking their wives to go to Hawaii or on a ski vacation or a Caribbean cruise. Eventually I said yes, a decision I lived to regret. The words "lived" and "regret," mind you, hold equal importance. In my opinion, any halibut trip a person survives is a success.

In part, I blame our Midwest upbringing. Jim had said, "After all, the family that works together stays together." He reminded me of all the farm families we had known, the wheat fields, the rolling rows of knee-high corn, and the long summer days with husband, wife, and all the children harvesting in the fields. It worked for them, right? We would just be harvesting fish.

One point I had neglected to consider was that commercial fishing represented a new career for Jim. My husband, our son Luke, and I would be far from home, on the water, with no one to consult for advice.

For that first trip out, I took vacation leave from my full-time job, bought my commercial deckhand license, and reported for "duty" on the *Kiviok*, our fishing boat.

We put on two layers of warm clothing, topped off with rain gear. I learned right quick how to plan ahead about going to the bathroom after discovering it took a good ten minutes to get off all the layers of clothing. This revelation came after the shock of being told the bathroom consisted of a five-gallon bucket sitting on the deck.

We proceeded to bait hooks after hauling anchors, hooks, groceries, clothing, bedding, and tubs to the boat (always at low tide). The baiting process took two days. I learned how to bait squid and herring on circle hooks and put them into a tub in a certain order so they can be removed easily and attached to the line going into the water—supposedly. Where we were headed to fish halibut, the setting and hauling of the line are allowed by regulation only in a set twenty-four-hour period. We then clean the fish and sell the catch to a larger boat called a "tender." It sounded simple.

While baiting, Jim and I battled over safety gear. My dear husband, the eternal optimist, knew for sure that nothing untoward would happen out on the high sea, so why waste precious time planning for some calamity? I prefer having a plan for every possible emergency. So I had bought survival suits; waxed the zippers; put candy bars, whistles and flashlight into the hands of the suits; and made everyone practice putting on the gear. I purchased flares and a life ring. I begged Jim to bring an extra VHF radio.

> Jim and I battled over safety gear. My husband, the eternal optimist, knew nothing untoward would happen on the high sea, so why waste precious time planning for a calamity?

Early Sunday morning and barely speaking, we cast off for Sumdum Bay, a twelve-hour trip. All went smoothly during daylight hours, but rather than stopping at night as advised, we plowed ahead into the darkness. About midnight we hit a submerged log. With no way to discern if the log had busted a hole in the bow, we propelled on northward through the choppy waters of Stevens Passage.

Eventually sleep overcame fear of sinking, and I awoke Monday morning at our destination.

"Gee, I didn't think there would be any ice in here this time of year," Jim says.

My beloved spouse had forgotten to mention the glacier in the bay. I felt as if I were in a giant punchbowl floating around among extremely large ice cubes. Many of the beautiful but dangerous icebergs were larger than houses. Any one of them, it seemed, could have punched a large hole in the boat.

At twelve o'clock sharp, the halibut fishery opened for twenty-four hours. The gear went out amid a lot of salty language. The ganions tangled in the tubs. I proceeded to get seasick, vomiting as gracefully as possible into the tubs with the tangled ganions. But, by gosh, I did not leave my post passing out hooks to the crabby captain.

After running out eighteen miles of gear, Luke and Jim ate. I devoured a seasick pill. We then began to haul in the gear. Well, let me tell you that anti-nausea medication does work, but it also puts a person to sleep. In fact, every time I sat, I fell asleep.

The memories do fade, but other well-remembered mishaps included getting line caught in the propeller as we backed up to avoid hitting an iceberg. We had a dilemma here. Jim had frowned on my suggestion to bring along a skiff as a safety measure, although every other boat had one. The twenty-four-hour halibut clock was tick, tick, ticking away. We needed to get the line and fish aboard, but the boat was dead in the water.

After Jim vetoed the skiff, I purchased a $32 "rubber raft for two." I think they meant two infants. It leaked air. I looked at Jim, all six feet, five inches and 300 pounds of him—a massive man who didn't know how to swim. I certainly felt he *deserved* to be the one to get into the raft and cut out the line. He looked at me and Luke. No way was I letting Luke get on that raft, so I was the one elected to get into the very tiny, leaky rubber raft and cut the line out of the propeller. I was so angry I forgot to be afraid. If Jim hadn't needed the line cut out so badly, I'm sure he would have been tempted to let go of the rope holding the raft.

Once the crisis was over, the anger passed. I remember the excitement as we caught many fish, including ten halibut weighing more than 300 pounds each. We could not pull them aboard, however, so we had to tie them to cleats on each side of the boat and keep on hauling gear. Time was running out.

We brought more fish aboard. The boat settled lower in the water. "You cannot bring another fish aboard this boat or we will sink!" I yelled at Jim. "Clear out the bunks," Jim replied. "I'll put them there." We kept hauling.

Finally we cleaned the fish. Some were so large, and I was so little, that I would use my head to hold the belly open to gut them. Just as I was thanking God that no one could see me covered in blood head to toe, tired, no make-up, no bath and very cranky, a float plane landed next to the boat. The president of Icicle Fisheries hopped aboard and says, "How you doing?" He was just dropping in for a visit. There was nowhere for me to hide. Has anyone ever died from acute embarrassment?

The fish delivered, we headed home. As the night lights of Petersburg came into view, the engine quit. We were out of fuel. I was tempted to leave Jim there and swim to town. Eventually a boat of drunken halibut fishermen towed us to town. After forty straight sleepless hours of hard work, I would have gone with anyone who promised a bath and a bed.

The next day, after a bath and eight hours of rest, the trip began to seem more like an adventure. The money in the bank looked good. It was fun to be down on the docks hearing everyone's story about their own misadventures. I began remembering only the good parts—the glacier, the icebergs, the whales, the porpoises following the bow of the boat and the excitement as we shouted "Halibut!" and gaffed each fish aboard. It was a good way for a family to become closer, and we did work well together.

So in spite of more crises, Jim continues to invite me on the yearly halibut trips. I continue to say yes.

SONJA JEAN WHITETHORN, born in 1948, lives in Petersburg in southeast Alaska and spends time each winter in Thousand Palms, California. She has a son who fishes and a daughter who is an English teacher. A retired registered nurse and a commercial halibut fisherman, Sonja finds kinship with her grandmother who homesteaded alone near the Black Hills of South Dakota, living in a sod shanty. The best thing about rural Alaska, she says, is "the relaxed lifestyle, the willingness of people to help one another in times of need, and the awesome beauty."

Clarence Wood looks for game.

17

∗ ∗ ∗ ∗ ∗ ∗ ∗ ∗ ∗ ∗ ∗

~ AMBLER ~

Gone fishin' up the Pah River
Steve W. Pilz

"**YOU'RE NOT GONNA BELIEVE IT** up there," says my friend, Nick Jans, who's just returned from up the Pah River, 160 miles upstream.

When Nick's more excited than usual, I can tell fish are involved. At the time, he and I had been casting lures up and down the Kobuk River in northwest Alaska for six years.

"Reallllly big pike up there," Nick says. "Chris caught one close to twenty pounds, I figure. Forty-three inches. You want to go or not?"

"Sure," I say. "How many did you get all together?"

"About a hundred," Nick says.

"Get the hell outta here."

"Okay, 200. You coming along or what?"

He knew what I'd answer.

Pike, *family esocidae*, are like no other freshwater fish. They are eating machines, pure and simple, and big ones at that. The muskellunge, largest of the class, tops out around seventy pounds. Next largest is the Northern Pike, which can reach fifty pounds. A rundown of the pike's diet tells you something. Young pike feed on small crustaceans, insects, and smaller pike. A large pike eats about anything: blackfish, burbot, suckers, whitefish, other pike, shore birds, small ducks, muskrats, mice, shrews, and crayfish.

It's no surprise, then, that pike don't spook easily. Even fishing from shore, I can roust a pike from its spot in the grass along the bank, only to have it turn and strike a lure. Pike are not a fish easily scared off by a passing boat, as dolly vardens can be. One pike after another can be hooked from the same spot on a river, lake or slough, no matter how much the previous fish thrashed around.

Because pike are not particularly territorial, many fish—even large ones-often can be found in a few square feet of prime habitat. Just as pike eat a variety of food, they will also take a variety of lures and live baits. Experts say that pike learn to avoid artificial lures, and while this may be true to a certain extent, I've caught numerous pike with the same spoon, including one with a lure of mine dangling from its lip. They apparently can't tell the difference between live bait on a hook and a small fish. A strip of baitfish or an artificial strip-bait on a spoon is most effective.

Nick and I have fished for pike on the tributaries of the Kobuk River both above and below Ambler, an Iñupiaq Eskimo village. We've poked around every promising slough we could find and even found schools of resident fish on the main river. This is what Nick calls a "find."

"How many times have we come up empty?" he asks. "This is a sure thing—if they're still there."

He says that before I can, because we both know that there are no guarantees in fishing, ever.

The Pah River lies mostly below the Arctic Circle, its headwaters far to the southeast amid a maze of wilderness lakes and sloughs into what's called "Indian" country—toward the Koyukuk River and on into interior Alaska. An old travel route that only the elder Eskimos know well, the Pah is known for large beavers harvested at high water in the spring. Local basket makers carve birch bark from the tall, straight trees on the river's banks. The ancient Iñupiat and Athabascans used to travel the Pah from the Interior to the arctic. Today, a four-hour boat trip takes us from Ambler to the mouth of the Pah, with the Iñupiaq villages of Shungnak and Kobuk and a dozen Eskimo fish camps in between.

Once into the Pah, the water turns dark and the channel narrows. The Lockwood Hills close in for a few miles before falling away and the Interior region opens wide.

Nick and I plan our trip for the first or second week of August, just before school starts.

The rain brings me back to earth, all three weeks of it. Not just any rain, but the most in forty years, the elders say. Interior villages on the other side of the mountains to the east, maybe 200 miles away on the Koyukuk, have been washed downstream. People are relocated to other villages or all the way to Fairbanks. On the Kobuk River, a German rafter, on vacation, drowned in an accident in the Kobuk's upper canyons. The water reaches flood stage in Ambler, and while people have seen the river that high in the spring, few can remember it being so high in the fall. Photos in *The Arctic Sounder*, the northwest arctic's weekly newspaper, show people in Kobuk floating past the post office in their boats.

Nick and I do catch some salmon and dolly varden and even grayling downriver. As we wait for this deluge to end, I'm convinced we won't see the Pah this year. Nick has no reason to believe we will, either. And so we wait.

School starts. I walk home in the rain for weeks. I start to ask about the Pah. Clarence Wood, preeminent Iñupiaq hunter around these parts, passes by me one day. I ask him when he was last up the Pah.

"Nick and I are going there," I say.

"Sure would like to *malik* (come along)," Clarence tells me. "Usually go there in springtime for beavers, real fa-a-a-t."

Clarence accentuates the last word as he recalls this Iñupiaq delicacy.

"Maybe you'll follow, Clarence, if this ever stops," I say, pointing to the sky. "You ever fish up there, Clarence?" I ask. He looks at me incredulously, squinting through his wet, dark glasses.

"Black bear up there," he says, "Maybe we'll get."

I know better than to ask Clarence about fish, but I had to know what he knew. But I wasn't about to find out, not today.

"Maybe whitefish up there," he cackles, peering at me over his glasses, his face breaking into a shitty grin. He laughs from deep in his belly. I wrinkle my nose to tell him what I think of his whitefish story. He knows I'm after something better. He's talked to Nick.

Clarence will *malik*, Nick tells me, because we're going, and it would be rude to head that way without him, to a place where Clarence was raised, without asking him to go. I'm as much a guest as Clarence but Nick seeks my input anyway. He knows Clarence will get bored with our fishing, but they're good friends. I tell Nick it's the fishing I'm interested in. Clarence can follow.

The rain stops and the river recedes. The morning temperatures dip into the low teens. It's mid-September and ice will come down the river in a couple weeks. Clarence makes his daily call. "Time to go, I guess, lot of black bear up that way."

"Even whitefish, eh, Clarence?" I say.

Clarence roars his laugh into the receiver. "Gotta call that bugger (Nick). Good night."

We plan our trip for the weekend. Take off on Friday after school and take Monday off work. We'll pick up Clarence above Kobuk at Vera and Leonard Douglas' fish camp. Clarence will take his wife, Marie, that far and set gill net for salmon, whitefish, sheefish, and anything else that swims along.

"Maybe whitefish up there," Clarence cackles, peering over his glasses, breaking into a shitty grin. He laughs from deep in his belly. He knows I'm after something better than whitefish.

The weather is uncooperative, the forecast worse. After school Friday, we're gone with thirty-five gallons of gas and enough food for a week. This is our last vacation until Christmas and we want to take full advantage of the days off.

We stop in Shungnak after two hours to visit friends. The conversation is about our destination, our summers, and how many caribou we saw on the way. Standard chitchat. Mention of the Pah brings talk about trout, sheefish, nice country, and how lucky we are to be going there. The Pah isn't easy to get to and it's a long way to go. A lot of people want to go. Few do.

It's getting dark. Next stop Kobuk, about thirty minutes on the river. We need gas for the rest of the trip and this is the last place to get it. Nick called ahead, so Eugene the Russian is waiting for us when we arrive. We get about thirty more gallons, paying an outrageous price. It was a monopoly extraordinaire in this Eskimo village of sixty.

"You'll be open on Monday?" Nick asks Eugene.

"I'm always here," Eugene replies in a thick Russian accent. "I'll see you Monday."

Darkness catches us a few bends upriver. Nick and I make a few casts from the boat after we set up the tent. We're looking for sheefish, but it's all but dark. The splash of our heavy metal spoons on the river breaks the almost silent flow of the river.

Saturday morning. Today we'll reach the Pah. We've got to get Clarence at Vera and Leonard's fish camp. It's a half hour from where we camped and about forty minutes from Kobuk.

I'm looking forward to getting to Vera and Leonard's. They'll know about the Pah. They've lived in Shungnak all their lives and are now in their sixties. There will be plenty of coffee, dried caribou and moose meat, seal oil, cookies and friendly conversation. Vera and Leonard are some of the most generous people I've ever known.

A moose carcass lays on the beach a bend above the camp. Clarence and Leonard have been at work. The moose walked through camp and Leonard, finishing his morning coffee, was late getting to it. He dropped it on the other side of the river. Clarence quickly skinned and cut it up.

I hadn't seen Vera or Leonard in three or four years. After hellos and a personal re-acquaintance, Nick asks Vera about the Pah, and pike.

"*Silik* (pike) up there anytime, I guess, but fall time, real fat," she says, accentuating her last word, just as Clarence did, telling us that this is the kind of fish she considers the best. Leonard listens on, looking Nick and me up and down wondering, I'm sure, why we would come all this way just to fish.

"*Naluagmiu* (white people) thing to do," Leonard says with a laugh, and a quick glance at his wife. We know he's just poking fun. We know it's his way of accepting us here in his home.

"Nothing but alligator (pike) up Pah," says Leonard. "Maybe

birch-bark or beaver in the spring. Now only alligator."

"Then we'll get us some of that kind," Nick says, slapping his knee for effect, making it clear we don't care what anyone thinks. We're going after big pike and no one's going to stop us.

We've long since stopped worrying about what people say when we head out on a fishing trip. "You're going where?" is a common thing to hear when I announce this to someone else. "What are you going to do there?" Fish, of course. What else?

This is like no other place I know. It's Alaska, and the fishing can be spectacular. Try fishing for sheefish until your arms get tired. Catch dolly varden that leap from the water six or seven times before they're landed. Salmon that feel like river-bottom snags until they start moving away from you. Nick and I have talked in circles about this stuff, and never seem to get tired of it.

Clarence knows we're antsy to get going, and he starts to put on his coveralls. He's eager to see a black bear, but more so just to get away from the camp and into his backyard, the country, which he knows like no one else.

We take turns hauling moose parts from Leonard's boat to under a tarp where the women will work for hours cutting the meat and putting it in Ziploc bags to take to Shungnak. We're promised moose meat on our return since we turn some down for now. Clarence grimaces but it's not his trip to say and he defers to the fishermen this time. We'll be eating fish, is how Nick puts it.

An hour and a half up the Pah, there is no sign of life on this horseshoe-shaped lake, accessible by a strip of water just wide enough for the boat to pass. It's easy to see why pike would live here, but our first two dozen casts bring nothing. Clarence lounges in the bow of the boat, amused by our intensity and bad language. We decide to set camp.

Nick and I say little. We know we haven't given the fishing enough time but quietly worry that something is amiss in the pike world. We collect wood for the fire and snack on whatever each of us drags from our packs. "Gotta be out there somewhere, Clarence." Nick says, "We'll be back in a little while." This is what I wanted to hear and head slowly to the boat, although I want to run.

"Yea, little while, Clarence."

Three hours later, Nick and I return with a couple fish a bit over ten pounds and a big one that Nick caught, just over seventeen pounds. Clarence is unimpressed. He shrugs when Nick hauls it from the boat. Nick says it's for his wall at home, and I'm jealous as hell.

More of the same in the morning makes the trip a resounding success with most fish at ten pounds or so, and several over fifteen.

Clarence has the tent dismantled and most of the gear lined up along the bank. This is hard to ignore, but I don't say a word. Neither does Nick. We're on a roll and the fish are in a frenzy, striking on almost every cast. Large wakes in the water tell us fish are on their way to our lures and we brace ourselves for a strike, time and time again. Nick says we better go. We'll sneak in a few casts on the way out, he promises, and if it goes like it has, it's another hour of fishing.

We load the boat and push off again. Nick says he needs to check the motor, make some adjustments, and add oil. He looks at me and says he'd fish if he were me. I agree, knocking off two more ten pounders, splashing water all over Clarence in the process. He grins. I feel better, thinking that he agrees with our tenacity and perseverance, if nothing else.

We slowly motor through the narrow channel that leaves the lake. I'm mostly satisfied but wanted a wall fish too. We've caught about fifty fish and kept six for the long winter. There's a creek flowing into the Pah just as we leave the channel. An eddy swirls lazily where the creek and the river meet. I grab my rod and reel and the anchor at the same time. Nick cuts the engine.

"Didn't notice this before. Water was too high." Nick says.

"I did," I say. "Let's try it."

Nick catches ten fish in the half hour we're there, all close to ten pounds and all leaping and running and thrashing around the boat or under it, making the pike population proud. The water here is not stagnant like in the lake and the fish are vigorous. I catch six or seven in the same time. Just before we're going to leave, I hit one that I can't get off the river bottom. There are no salmon or sheefish here, and I know it must be big. I try again and feel it swim ever so slowly, heavily away from me, and then faster as the drag on the reel sings.

"Get the net!" I yell to Nick.

The fish runs for the boat. I realize I'll lose him. I plunge my rod tip into the water and mentally cross my fingers, hoping it doesn't drag the line over a sharp edge on the boat or something in the river. It sinks again and hunkers on the bottom. I'm determined to make it rise again to tire it out but don't want to horse it. With all the stress my ten-pound test line has taken, it won't last much longer. I feel the fish come off the bottom again and rush for the shallow water of the creek. I let him go, as if I have a choice, hoping he won't break the water and spit the hook. It stops just short of the bank and the creek, giving me a chance to try to turn it back towards the boat. It must be tiring, because as the drag stops and I pull a little, I feel it sink into the eddy without running. I start to reel and feel it come. "The net, Nick!" It's only been five minutes, but I'm not taking any chances. It might have more life, but I don't want to know. Nick makes his standard announcement: "You want to net him already?"

"Net the son-of-a-bitch if he comes up this time," I yell. "My line can't take much more."

And even if I had fresh line, I'd have wanted that fish now, because if it wasn't tired, I was, and I can sport fish some other day. This one was going home.

Maybe it was tired or knew it was time for us to head out, but that eighteen-pound pike slid into the net and Nick hoisted it into the boat. "There," he said. "All yours. Nice fish."

"Thanks—had to have that one." I say.

"So I noticed," Nick says.

"Thanks."

"Time for that black bear, Clarence?" Nick asks.

Clarence grins. "You guys done already?" he asks.

"'Til next time," answers Nick.

It's late afternoon as we reel in our lines and start to float down the Pah toward the fish camps and a good place to spend the night. We ready the boat for travel, securing things that might bounce out or blow away. I wonder when I'll get back to the Pah and if the alligators will still be here. I know they will and I'll be back except this is fishing with no guarantees.

I'd go back whether there were fish or not, which is a funny thing for a fisherman to say.

STEVE W. PILZ, born in 1961, lives in Wisconsin. When he taught school in Kivalina on Alaska's northwest arctic coast, his students asked if he had a nickname. He told them that when he played basketball, he was called "Iceman," after a professional basketball player. This led to his Iñupiaq name, Siku, meaning "ice," which took on more relevance in Ambler when he spent much time fishing through the ice of the Kobuk River. He and his wife, Venita, an Iñupiaq, have two children. Besides living in Kivalina, he taught school in Ambler where his family "picked berries, set net for salmon, and harvested caribou." He has a bachelor of science degree in English from the University of Wisconsin, Stevens Point. In retirement, he coaches youth football, basketball, and baseball, and is a freelance sportswriter.

Caribou swim Onion Portage in northwest Alaska.

18

* * * * * * * * * * * *

~ KOTZEBUE ~

Caribou hunting on the Kobuk River
Emma Snyder

CARIBOU HUNTING IS HARD WORK. I try to leave it to the experts, such as my husband, Jackson. My son (when he was young) and I like the easy part of hunting, which is to shoot the caribou, but not necessarily the butchering part. This may gross out some people, including animal-lovers, but this is our way of life in northwest Alaska.

We usually travel from Kotzebue up the Kobuk River to go hunting each year in early September. This is a two- to three-day trip. We usually spend the night with relatives in Kiana, one of ten villages surrounding Kotzebue. Kiana is about sixty miles up the river from Kotzebue.

By Labor Day, the leaves on the willows have turned yellow and orange. The tundra is mostly flat with animals moving about including moose, bears, and muskrat. There are also blueberries, blackberries, and cranberries to pick. At this time of year, the river is usually glassy calm during the daylight. At night, the moonlight shadows the river with orange and red colors on the water. Farther upriver, tall green spruce trees and birch trees begin to appear, a change from the treeless arctic coast. The caribou migrate from the north, passing through the hills and across the Kobuk River to the area where they mate and look for food. The caribou's most important food is moss.

During a successful hunt, we can catch at least five caribou in one place, such as where a herd crosses the river. This represents a winter's supply of meat for a whole family. We wait until the herd has begun to cross in deep enough water before shooting them in the neck, killing them instantly.

"Son, aim to the neck," instructs my husband, Jackson.

"Now get that other bull! Hurry!" shouts Mom.

I can't aim right. Taking off my jacket for a better position, I try to aim directly for the neck. As the rifles go off with a loud bang, I understand feeling sorry for hurting the animals, but I remember the caribou's fat meat that is so delicious to eat

During a successful hunt, we can catch five caribou in one place, such as where a herd crosses the river. This represents a winter's supply of meat for a whole family.

"Okay, now, let's tie up the horns," my husband says. "Good shot, son."

Our son, Charles, starts to count one, two, three, four.

"How many more are we going to hunt, Dad?" Charles asks.

The caribou are tied by the antlers and dragged to the shore for butchering. My husband starts to skin the caribou while my son and I look out for more caribou. With a sharp knife, he starts on the breast part of the carcass, cutting down to the end of the stomach. At the same time, he tries not to puncture the stomach. If he does, the caribou will become quite messy and hard to clean.

After that's done, my husband starts the process of parting the skin from the stomach area on one side down toward the rib cage. He then does the same for the other side. After that, he carefully punctures a hole below the breast big enough to stick two fingers through to guide the knife all the way down to the stomach. At this point, the stomach is pulled out of the rib cage. Then he takes out the heart and liver and the fat that separates the intestines from the belly, as well as a few more parts to be cleaned and put aside. The elders like to eat certain parts of the caribou as a delicacy, such as the tongue, which is quite tasty.

The stomach area now is ready to be cleaned with water, and

the skin of the caribou is ready to be removed. The second major step in skinning the caribou involves cutting at the hind legs, from the hoofs up toward the butt area and then moving over to the front legs to do the same. The head is either removed at the site or kept on until reaching home. I would imagine this is no different from butchering a cow down in the Lower 48. The only difference is that it's more likely done in a butcher shop there.

After reaching Kotzebue, we all chip in to put away the meat by cutting it up into pieces that fit gallon-size Ziploc bags to be stored in a freezer for winter use. My husband usually delivers some meat to neighbors and relatives who live in Kotzebue. Sometimes, we bring a carcass to the store to have the meat cut up for steaks, stews, and ground meat. This way, we don't need to spend too much money on chicken and other meat products over the winter.

Caribou hunting is part of the Iñupiaq livelihood. Our ancestors have been hunting and surviving on caribou for centuries. This is one main source of food that we cannot go without. Our parents taught us how to hunt. My husband and I are teaching our children to hunt. No matter what anyone says about our culture, no one can change that. I cannot speak for other cultures. We all have our different ways of living.

I'm thankful that I am an Iñupiaq Eskimo.

Emma Snyder and her husband, Jackson

EMMA IVALU STALKER SNYDER, born in 1958, is an Iñupiaq who lives in Kotzebue but was born in Noatak in northwest Alaska. A mother of five children, Emma has been married to Jackson Snyder since August 1983. Growing up she was the only girl among ten brothers. "I grew up traveling by dog team from different villages for subsistence purposes," she recalls. "My father was a reindeer herder." She works as special assistant to the board of directors of NANA, the Native regional corporation in northwest Alaska. In recent years, Emma adopted a foster child and finished a three-year Bible program. She also has taken social services coursework.

Historic photo of elder with children

*

GENERATIONS

IN RURAL ALASKA, Native people almost universally live around their extended family, while non-Native families, often come from other places, and often do not have extended family nearby. Some non-Natives either have married into Native families or established multi-generational ties in certain rural communities such as Nome.

In the early 1980s in northwest Alaska, Iñupiaq Eskimos faced deteriorating conditions among their people after decades of social upheaval from western and other outside influences. They came together to address serious social problems after realizing that young Natives in particular were struggling between two worlds, aboriginal and Western.

In their quest for solutions, the Iñupiat identified seventeen values that had sustained them as a people since time immemorial: sharing, humility, hard work, spirituality, cooperation, family roles, domestic skills, love for children, respect for nature, respect for others, respect for elders, responsibility to tribe, knowledge of language, knowledge of family tree, hunter success, humor, and avoidance of conflict. This program is called Iñupiat *Ilitqusiat*, which means "the Real People's gathering place of wisdom and knowledge."

In addition to those values, the Iñupiat, like Native Americans throughout the continent, also identified a traditional Iñupiaq value that has endured across the many thousands of years that they have called the Far North their home: a special esteem and respect for tribal elders.

Of course, non-Natives in Alaska, as elsewhere, pay homage to their elders, too. This section explores several generations of rural Alaskans as they interact and as they absorb and pass on en-during values, no matter the location, no matter the situation.

John Creed returns to the village where he had been a young schoolteacher and expresses his gratitude to the widow of a caring elder who had helped him out of a tight spot years before.

Susan Andrews describes simply trying to walk from work to home to breast-feed her first baby one day in Kotzebue when an arctic blizzard forces her to crawl back to the office after becoming disoriented in a blinding whiteout. She also describes walking in Kotzebue with her late grandmother, who at the time was eighty-two and lived to be ninety-six.

Another esteemed elder, the late Della Keats, remains one of Alaska's most famous tribal doctors decades after her death at seventy-nine in 1986. It's the story of a remarkable woman who left a legacy of traditional Native healing that has endured into the new millennium and likely will inspire many generations to come. Ruthie Tatqavin Sampson was a prominent Iñupiaq scholar whose legacy also promises to continue celebrating and advancing Iñupiaq language and culture in northwest Alaska well into the future.

Finally, Sonja Whitethorn writes about a truth that all parents share: our children will find their own path in life despite our own dreams and wishes for them, and they may well succeed beyond our expectations.

John Creed gathers water by
snowmachine in Noatak in 1980.

19

* * * * * * * * * *

~ NOATAK ~

Return to an arctic village
John Creed

IT WAS FALL CARIBOU-HUNTING SEASON in Noatak, the Iñupiaq community where I used to teach, primarily English, to middle- and high-school students.

The caribou typically migrate close to the village this time of year, when just about everybody's boat on the river teems with fresh red meat and tangles of antlers. Caribou hangs on racks. Caribou carcasses lie in rows outside local homes. Caribou fills freezers.

It was 1979 when I first set foot in this isolated settlement on the banks of the Noatak River in northwest Alaska that I once called home as a young schoolteacher. Today I live out on the arctic coast in the region's "big city," Kotzebue. My return to Noatak had taken more than a decade.

"Hey, JC! Remember me?"

I was approached by a few young men and women in their twenties as I walked through the village. So many of these former students I could have sworn I'd never seen before.

"I'm John Williams," said one tall, trim young man who had noticed me walking down to the riverbank one morning.

"John Williams? You used to be a little guy," I said, remembering how he and I spent hours in a makeshift darkroom in the school's bathroom, printing photographs for Noatak's first-ever school yearbook. John was now maintaining Noatak's oil-fired electric power plant.

I also ran into Frank Onalik, another former student. Frank said he got some training in operating heavy equipment in Seward on the Kenai Peninsula and would like to work at the nearby Red Dog Mine, site of one of the world's richest lead and zinc deposits. The mine had started up a few years before.

I chatted with Mary Arey, Noatak's long-time postmistress and daughter of distinguished elder "Aana Nellie" Woods. I told Mary I had run into her daughter, Pearl, a former student who loved to read, on the University of Alaska campus in Fairbanks a few years before. Pearl became a certified teacher. Pearl and her husband still were plugging away at their degrees in Anchorage while making a living and raising their young children. (Pearl did become a certified teacher and then worked for the oil industry. Tragically, she died of heart failure in 2009.)

In Noatak, I had rented Harold Downey's house, though I'd never met him. He was spending the winter working on Barter Island east of Prudhoe Bay on Alaska's North Slope. Nevertheless, I'd always wanted to meet this man whose hand-crafted, oil-drum woodstove had kept me warm all winter, and whose traditional Eskimo tools I'd admired, such as the one for digging roots with the steel head and the handle carved from a caribou or moose antler. I'd always wanted to tell him how much I marveled at the way he made his Noatak home so comfortable.

Here was my chance. He was standing on his small porch, as straight and erect as a man thirty or forty years younger. As I approached, he greeted me with a big smile. I had to yell my name into his ear, but even if he heard it, it wouldn't have mattered. He spoke only Iñupiaq.

"I lived in your house a few years ago," I told him. He smiled. "It's a good house, ah, a nice house," I said. He smiled again.

I studied the face of this ancient gent who had been born in a time before there had been much outsider contact.

Next to Harold lived Nellie Woods, my former next-door neighbor and another legendary Noatak elder. Nellie was still smiling, still getting around, and still hooking fish through the river ice each winter. I couldn't tell if she remembered me, as she greeted everyone with equal warmth, but I sure remembered

Nellie, an extraordinary woman who helped drive a reindeer herd along the coast of the Arctic Ocean in the 1930s to help Native Iñuit in northern Canada.

Walking back toward the school, I passed through Barbara Wesley's yard, where she was cutting and hanging caribou. Her dear and generous husband, Floyd Wesley Sr., had passed away. Floyd had managed the Noatak Native Store for many years.

"I sure miss him," Barbara said. "He sure spoil me. Always make me coffee. I guess I get more used to him gone now."

"Floyd was a fine man," I said, and proceeded to tell her why I'd always thought that.

Even though I was merely one teacher in a long string of teachers passing through Noatak, Floyd Wesley was unfailingly friendly and witty and helpful to me the whole time I lived in the village. In the spring, for example, when I would go to the river to get water, I'd sink up to my crotch in the soft snow. Floyd showed me where water was coming right out of the ground close by.

He also defended me once.

"One time Floyd helped me in a big way," I told his widow.

On a clear sunny evening in March of my first year in the Arctic, I was chopping firewood in front of my house. I had noticed earlier in the day that one of the young men in the village had been drinking. I had avoided him then, even though I didn't figure he'd be a problem. He had visited my place many times.

Even when I saw him walking toward me that evening, I wasn't too concerned, especially with an axe in my hand—until he walked right through me, pushing me, and kicking the axe out of my hand.

"You teachers think you're such big shots!" he roared, eyes bulging with rage. I tried to get into my house. He blocked the way. I turned and started toward the school—quickly but not running.

He jumped on my back, wrapping his forearm across my throat, pulling me to the ground backwards. I did not resist. I looked up at the sky as my arms dangled by my side.

Floyd was cutting up a seal in front of his house. When he saw what was happening, he rushed over.

"You leave this teacher alone—now go on!" commanded Floyd. He was obeyed immediately. Floyd made sure the young man left the area, whereupon Floyd returned to his work but not before shooting me a reassuring glance. I thanked him in a whisper.

I didn't want to, but I went right back to chopping wood as word sped through the village. "Hey, JC, what's going on, man?" my students asked as they approached from all directions, wondering whether there might be some more action.

"Just gettin' some wood chopped," I replied nonchalantly, smiling calmly.

Out of the corner of my eye, though, I could see my attacker approaching again, this time with a friend.

"Now there are two of them," I thought.

I started shaking inside as they approached, but I had to stay steady as my students watched. The two young men broke through the knot of little kids standing around the chopping block and walked straight to me. Was I about to get pummeled?

"I'm sorry, man," my attacker said, his eyes squinting downward. "I'm really sorry."

I put my arms around him. I said I thought he was a good guy. His anger and frustration had to go somewhere; a few minutes earlier, I just happened to be a convenient target. It was nothing personal.

The young man reeled back on his heels, squeezed his eyes closed, clenched his fists, and wailed at the sky.

"I want to kill myself!" he cried, tears streaming down his cheeks.

Minutes before, I had feared for my safety, yet that could not compare with the constant pain this young man endured every day.

Now, a decade later, I was standing on the same spot where

the late Floyd Wesley had stood when he realized I needed help.

"Floyd was a good man," I told Barbara Wesley, Floyd's widow, as she hung caribou on her drying rack.

JOHN CREED is a professor of journalism and humanities at the University of Alaska's Chukchi College in Kotzebue, where he has distance taught site-bound students throughout Alaska since 1987. Before joining the UA faculty, he covered business and education for the *Fairbanks Daily News-Miner.*

A snowstorm and whiteout conditions diminish visibility in Kotzebue.

20

* * * * * * * * * * *

~ KOTZEBUE ~

Beating around the bush on foot
Susan B. Andrews

I'M LIKE A DOG. I need my daily walk. But this pastime carries with it a certain amount of risk in bush Alaska. For instance, one morning I walked to work as usual, only to find the main door locked. "Huh? Nobody here today?"

It did seem colder than usual, but not *that* much colder. I pulled my ruff tighter around my face so the hood looked like a periscope, then headed back home. I checked the temp by calling the weather service. Wind chill: 108 below zero. Work had been cancelled. It scared me that I'd stumbled into that kind of weather unaware.

I blame my maternal grandmother, Rosamond Baldwin. She passed the walking-fever gene on to me. We were always close, though a half-century separated us. (Perhaps I should consider myself old enough now to guard the truth about my exact age as if that bit of knowledge were a favorite family recipe, but I really don't mind divulging that my grandmother was born in 1909 and I in 1959.)

A continent separated us, too. Her home was on the Upper East Side of Manhattan and mine was on the Upper northwest side of North America, specifically in Kotzebue, twenty-six miles above the Arctic Circle. The universe doesn't get much more urban than in New York City nor much more rural and remote than the arctic. Yet, we both lived in a pedestrian-friendly environment. She got around her "village" on foot, as do I around mine.

At one time, she shared her one-room apartment with a sheltie dog named Sophie, who did not enjoy the same gift of longevity as her owner, even in dog years. But while Sophie was alive, her regular need for at least a curb if not a patch of grass or snow forced my grandmother to go out for a walk even on those rare occasions when she might not have felt like taking a walk— for instance, on a winter day when the city's towering high-rises corral the wind, leaving it nowhere to go but barreling through the city's thoroughfares. A favorite walk would take Gran, as grandchildren and great-grandchildren alike called her, along with her canine companion down a handful of city blocks to Gracie Mansion, home of the city mayor. There, in Carl Schurz Park, Sophie conducted her sniffing rituals with other New Yorkers' pets. Then the dogs might begin to romp, which typically served as a prelude to chatting between the pets' owners, whose mutual love of dogs swept away the usual suspicion and distrust of strangers in America's largest city.

Gran always embraced her four-footed friends as part of her spiritual life. For instance, she would make a point of attending an annual blessing of the animals at the Cathedral of Saint John the Divine in Manhattan.

In Kotzebue, the majority of dogs lead narrow lives at the end of a short chain, protecting property including snowmobiles, all-terrain vehicles, and homes. Others are kept for running in a dog team. Many local dogs are decidedly utilitarian, but our family dog, Kubla, qualified as a pet. Kubla was a black and white part-springer spaniel. My husband and I adopted Kubla as a puppy shortly after we were married.

Our dog was as pampered, if not as spoiled, as Gran's dog. Kubla also loved her daily walk, so much so that even on days with double-digit, below-zero wind chills, Kubla, John, and I still would take that routine morning stroll. It took roughly thirty minutes to make a round-trip to the Kotzebue post office.

Beforehand, when John and I would be pulling on insulated overpants, parkas, neck-warmer or face-mask, fleece-lined hats, goggles, polypropylene gloves and over-mitts, it was like Kubla responding to the ring of a bell for Pavlov's dog. Her conditioned response? Panting. In anticipation of going out into the frigid arctic cold? Curious.

Kubla's only "gear" was the hairy "feathering" fur that grew between her paws every winter as protection from the cold. We called these her "ptarmigan paws."

Susan Andrews with Kubla, the family dog,
on a trip to the Post Office.

John and I always could count on Kubla to trot a few paces ahead on the way to the post office. She moved noiselessly, her ptarmigan paws fluttering across the snow, while John and I could go nowhere without the distinct crunch, crunch, crunch of our footsteps marking our progress.

One blisteringly cold morning, when Kubla was in her fourteenth year, John and I were inching our way along a field by an in-town cemetery, raging wind at our faces. Kubla wasn't ahead of us this time; she barely was keeping pace. Her ears, with the silky black fur that always reminded me of a bad perm, were flattened back, exposing the delta of her ear canals. White hairs flecked her muzzle and around her eyes, a testament to the many winters she'd survived. Her belly had swelled in recent years from over-eating and from her favorite pastime, trash-picking. No one ever mistook her for a puppy now. A year or two earlier, she'd lost that springing step. Now her gait was tentative and stiff.

We continued on into the severe wind chill. Kubla had handled these conditions before. But she seemed to falter now. John pushed our bicycle cart converted into a stroller—handy for transporting children, groceries, mail, and packages across the only street in town that was paved at the time, Third Avenue. We were within striking distance of the P.O. now. Kubla limped forward, past the Friends Church, the largest denomination in the region.

We reached the P.O. Right there in the lobby, Kubla turned into a brick of cold. As if the warmth of the building had shocked her system, she suddenly looked like the cartoon character Wile E. Coyote after falling off a cliff in his never-ending pursuit of the roadrunner. Almost comical. But this wasn't funny. Kubla's body stood as rigid as a mast on a ship. I thought she might keel over right there, as if rigor mortis already had set in.

It seemed as if she was too cold to shiver. I reached for her.

"Kubla, it's okay," I whispered. "You're going to be okay."

Kubla's tail did not wag. She did not lean into me as usual when I stroked that gentle slope where her head met her neck. She could not move.

John and I waited for her to thaw. We caressed her ears and head some more. We decided that Kubla should ride home, then lifted her into the cart.

But no, our little old friend would not be babied. With this affront to her dignity, Kubla rallied, clambering out of the cart. So, when we left the post office, Kubla was willing to leave too. She kept up, sometimes even approximating a trot, the wind now at our back.

We snapped on the radio at home. We'd taken Kubla out in a wind chill of 100 degrees below zero. This was like taking your

Susan's parka-clad grandmother, Rosamond W. Baldwin,
during a visit to northwest Alaska.

grandmother out into treacherous weather on a walk. Oops, I
can't say I haven't done that, either.

Gran, at eighty-two, was the first member of my extended
family to visit Kotzebue. She arrived in April 1991, partly to
meet her namesake, our then-infant daughter, Tiffany Rosamond
Creed, whose middle name comes from her great-grandmother's
first name. We sometimes called Tiffany "T. Rosamond" to her
great-grandmother's delight.

By April every year, we have passed the vernal equinox, so
the days in arctic Alaska were stretching longer than those Gran
had left behind in New York. But snow and ice still coated the
roads in Kotzebue, along with huge drifts of brilliant white snow.

"How pure and clean!" she marveled. "The snow reminds
me of my childhood, back in Massachusetts, before automobiles
began spreading their soot around."

She peered out from the ruff on the parka I loaned her, ab-
sorbing the dazzling winter wonderland dancing all around her.

I checked and double-checked the tread on her boots. She couldn't afford a fall. She'd broken her hip in her late seventies. Although she'd recovered, except for a slight limp, she couldn't risk slipping on the hard-packed snow and ice.

An elderly woman's risk of fracturing a hip is great. Suddenly, Gran's life seemed so fragile, like a tiny moss clinging to a piece of granite back at her birthplace in New England. Luckily, the temperatures weren't forbidding. Above zero—no problem.

However, I hadn't accounted for the wind. We started out, not really noticing the breeze, her hand a mass of mitten in mine. Our mission? Walk from the house John and I and our children then called home to Chukchi College, a branch of the University of Alaska, where I worked. There I would introduce her to the folks at the office and show her the community library.

About halfway into this ten-minute trek, the wind kicked up. Gran had plenty of wraps to stay warm, but her grip tightened on my hand.

"Oh my," she whispered. "I think I'd better get more support."

She steadied herself by locking her arm around my elbow. She weighed more than I did.

"She'll go down with me if I slip," I thought. If one of us lost our footing, she could end up in the hospital.

This was only a walk, a simple walk, one I'd made so many times, but never did I expect it to introduce this kind of fear. The wind whipped around us like a lasso, and there was little solace in knowing that if that imaginary rope caught either of us around the foot, we'd go down together.

For the first time, the truth was blowing in my face: Gran, this precious person in my life, would not be around forever. Was it a mistake to invite her here?

For the first time in my life, the truth was blowing in my face: Gran, this precious person in my life, would not be around forever. Was it a mistake to have invited her here?

My strides shortened. I wasn't going to let her slip and fall.

I just wouldn't let it happen. Gran and I managed to arrive at the college without incident. I especially remember how she took to one of my colleagues, an education professor with a handsome puff of prematurely white hair. Perhaps it reminded her of the snows of yesteryear.

At this writing, my children (four of her thirteen great-grandchildren) are growing up or have grown up in a Native community, which holds its elders in the highest esteem. For this reason, I feel a particular kinship with the Iñupiaq value of respect for elders. Who would I be without Gran's enduring influence?

"The only things that really count in life are health and love," Gran once told me.

I have shared this bit of Gran's wisdom with all our children, including Myles, our oldest child, who also has been subject to the whims of nature. Take the time he was a baby and needed a nursing. Faced with another treacherous walk, I wasn't able to deliver because I was pitted against that much greater "mom" of us all, Mother Nature.

It was the darned weather again that brought danger during a walk in Kotzebue. A furious blizzard kicked up one day just before I was to head home from work to nurse Myles. I left the college amid the raging storm, stumbling through a snowdrift that used to be a street. Suddenly, I stopped short of crashing head-long into the invisible white walls of Kotzebue's National Guard Armory next door to the college. I struggled to get my bearings, the angled wind firing knife-like, stinging sleet at me.

In such extreme whiteout conditions, unusual even for Kotzebue, I was as invisible as everything around me, being swallowed up in a tempestuous whiteness. No real sense of up, down, forward, or back. If I stumbled and collapsed into a drift, or became disoriented, I might not be discovered until the storm cleared, perhaps not for another twenty-four hours or more.

I remembered with a shudder the story of a Kotzebue woman a few years before who'd wandered in circles to the point of exhaustion up on Cemetery Hill overlooking town. I'd heard about elders being lost in snowbanks right within the confines of town.

Now, here I was, considering these similar dangers, contemplating these similar risks. I, too, was trapped in one of these horridly similar arctic blizzards. But this was no heroic wilderness trek. Noble search-and-rescue troops would not be called out to find and deliver me back to safety. I was getting lost in a blizzard a mere 500 feet away from where I work.

I could have skipped lunch and stayed at work instead of trying to make it home at lunchtime, but Myles required my presence. He was home with John and needed to nurse. John and I at the time were switching off with our work schedules, day and night, so that I could continue to work and still nurse Myles every four hours or so.

Now it looked as if Myles either was going to have to learn to take a bottle from John, or cry out in hunger. Or, I could press on through this outrageous blizzard. The prospect of John's misery as he tried to cajole Myles into taking a bottle for the first time in his life compelled me to get home. Deeper into the mysterious whiteness I plodded.

I stumbled around, my feet punching through drifted snow that used to be a street. Or maybe it was the side of the road. I had no way of telling. My senses told me nothing. Everything felt the same to touch. The massive amounts of swirling snow muffled all sound. My goggles, all clouded and blurry, proved useless. I removed them. I could not see. The sleet stabbed my eyes, effectively blinding me.

A normally innocuous five-minute walk home for lunch had become a major threat.

Growing up, I had reason to fear the ocean, but I had no particular phobia about blizzards. It had never occurred to me to fear I might get caught in a whiteout. In clearer weather, I might have boasted, "I've taken this path home so many times, I could find my way home blindfolded." Now, I recognized nothing in my environment. I thought about the Iñupiat, who for 10,000 years in this harsh northern environment had no such man-made landmarks as a massive armory rising out of the frozen tundra and surrounded by similar large structures. How well they had to know the shape of every hill, every turn in the river, every spruce stump, every willow, the right time to travel, and most important, the right time to stay put and wait out the storm.

So, should I push on home where my baby was waiting anxiously to nurse? Should I return to my workplace? Either way, I could get lost. My breasts were heavy with milk, but the baby would have to wait. The college was much closer. I had a better shot at retracing my steps even though my footprints (more like leg prints punched through drifts) were filling in with blowing snow as quickly as I made them.

I turned back.

Struggling across snow a couple inches at a time, I hoped I was traveling in a straight line back to the college. I felt like Hansel and Gretel (okay, just Gretel) in a perverse, Kafkaesque fairy tale. It turned out I overshot the building a bit, but I finally found the entrance and dragged myself up the mound of snow that used to be stairs. With all the strength I had left, I pulled open the heavy red doors of the college and stumbled, exhausted, into the lobby.

"John. It's me," I said to my husband over the phone. "I'm back at the college. I couldn't get home! But it sounds like one of the Merrills can give me a ride home on a snowmachine when it clears a bit."

"How much longer?" John asked. In the background, I heard thunderous wails of Myles's misery.

"Did you try a bottle?"

"He won't take it."

My sense of triumph over Mother Nature in finding my way back to the comfort of the college was fleeting. In her grander scheme, I was a mere mammal needing to nurse her young.

Mother Nature undoubtedly will replay this same, familiar story of human vulnerability in the face of such awesome power over and over again across the years, but especially as we all get older. Indeed, Nature's inevitable trajectory meant that because of my grandmother's advanced age, my dear Gran, my walking inspiration, would be taken away, not just from me, but from the many generations who loved her so much and so well.

Afterword

Rosamond W. Baldwin slipped away peacefully in February 2006 on Valentine's Day, shortly after she was brought to a local hospital from her New York apartment, where she had lived independently until the last day of her long life. When she died this beloved family matriarch was just two weeks shy of her ninety-seventh birthday. May her spirit live on in all of us.

For her grandmother's memorial, Susan penned a poem that speaks to life's transience.

Rosamond

You and I ventured through the pasture to Lighthouse Beach.
It was low tide.
With a stick, I wrote your name "Rosamond" in the sand.
You smiled even though my lettering was uneven
    and imperfect.

We stood together and watched the tide creep in.
A seagull squawked overhead.
I looked upward.
When I turned back, you were gone—vanished.

I stood there alone and watched the tide roll in.
First, the water obscured your name in the sand.
Then it washed your name away completely
as if you had never existed.

I stood there, stunned, that nature
could take away something so precious.

The gull squawked again. I looked up.
Once it caught my attention, it flew away,
taking our grief with it.

SUSAN B. ANDREWS lives north of the Arctic Circle in Kotzebue, Alaska, with her husband, John Creed, and family. Susan is professor of journalism and humanities at the Kotzebue branch of the University of Alaska, Chukchi College, where she has taught since 1989. Before coming to Kotzebue, she was anchor and news director at the KTVF-TV, the CBS affiliate in Fairbanks.

Della Keats

21

* * * * * * * * * * * *

~ KOTZEBUE ~

Della Keats: pride of her people
John Creed

HER PEOPLE LOVED HER DEARLY and depended on her for decades. By her late seventies, she'd worked her entire life— quietly and mostly for no pay—in the dozen or so remote Iñupiaq Eskimo villages that dot the vast arctic wilderness in northwest Alaska.

Many Iñupiat—the "Real People"—knew her simply as Putyuk, her Iñupiaq name. ("Iñupiat" refers to the people. "Iñupiaq" refers to the language and individuals.) To the rest of the world, she was Della Keats, the renowned Eskimo doctor.

Many believe Della in her lifetime was the revered heir to the rich legacy of traditional Iñupiaq medicinal practices. She helped sick and injured people her whole life without fanfare, using techniques learned from a variety of sources.

"I feel it with my hands, just with my hands," said Della, explaining about how she examines her patients.

She would search the body for abnormalities with hands so strong she could move the muscles of the strongest of men. So sensitive she could turn a breached baby or follow along a person's insides, probing for trouble. She then would apply one of her methods—developed over six decades—to the cure. Then she would show the patient, or members of his or her family, how to treat the problem themselves.

Those animated hands, always in motion, helped her speak.

Many people, especially elders, preferred Della to western

doctors. She was one of the people. She spoke Iñupiaq. Her patients relaxed. They contrasted Della's warmth and knowledge with doctors they hardly knew. Who poked and probed with cold, sterile instruments. Who diagnosed from X-rays and the like.

Della treated an array of ailments: arthritis, infected kidneys, injured joints, and sprains, to name a few.

As for medicine, many of her cures came from arctic plants, including one in particular that the Iñupiat, to this day, call *sargigruaq*. But even in Iñupiaq country, it's commonly known as "stinkweed." Della prescribed broth boiled from the leaves for "sour stomach"—heartburn, colds, and respiratory troubles. Infections are soaked in the solution.

Della started administering her own remedies as a young woman. The middle child of seven, she was born in a moss hut in 1907, four miles upriver from her home village of Noatak in northwest Alaska. Her mother's method of giving birth is long defunct, as are so many traditional practices of Della's people, who have followed the fish, the game, and the seasons since time immemorial, dictated by one of the planet's most severe, unforgiving climates.

For many years most Iñupiaq women have delivered their babies at the modern hospital in Kotzebue, northwest Alaska's hub of trade and commerce. Toward the final years of her life, that suited Della just fine.

"Maybe I get some sleep sometimes," she says, then laughs from the gut.

Radical changes in birthing practices symbolize an extraordinary journey for Della's people, these once ever-moving bands of arctic hunters and fishers—a journey spanning centuries of living within the harsh, relentless rhythms of this far north land.

Only in recent centuries did Della's people make contact with European culture. Tremendous change followed. Whatever the past, Della carried another time and culture in her hands, in her mind, within her heart. But she blended the past with the present in hopes for the most modern of futures. Her extensive experience, research, and love drew from the dominant western culture as well as her own. "Della's knowledge is becoming current," many western doctors said during her lifetime, an acknowledgement of the broadening of their own medical practices.

It was always difficult to define Della despite the western obsession for scientific measure. But Della would be the first to tell anyone sternly that she was no shaman; that is, if you're foolish enough to ask about shamans. Like many Natives of her day, she was uncomfortable with the subject. Iñupiaq shamans possessed supernatural powers. At one time they exerted enormous influence over the people—until Christianity arrived, after which the shamans' influences weakened dramatically.

Like most Iñupiaq, Della always took pains to distance herself from any "religion" practiced before Christianity swept into her homeland in the early 1900s. Beyond any doubt, today Christianity remains the mainstay in the Iñupiaq spiritual diet, reigning from frame and log churches in every regional village, from the collective soul of a sharing people.

Where did Della fit in the medical world? In the outside world's daunting search for absolutes, Della perhaps best fit the description of western culture's "natural" healers—those who don't necessarily reject all the drugs and machinery of modern western medicine (as Della also never did), but treat sickness and injury beyond just the symptom level but in relation to the total person: diet, exercise, life style, environment, drug and alcohol consumption, stress, occupation. A natural healer's treatment is not primarily a prescription to fill, some pills to take. It can range from therapeutic massage to a whole grain-based diet to acupuncture to chiropractic care. Della told people, over and over again, that she was neither a mystic nor a "faith" healer.

"You know," she said, "I just try to help them peoples, and just try to be quiet, and they call me a 'healer.' I learn it just by work on the patients, even though they call me a superstition lady, but I have none—only faith in my good Lord."

The "old ways" in the modern world never died, though they have undergone a considerable metamorphosis. Western-style organizations such as Kotzebue-based Maniilaq Health Center, run as a regional non-profit health and social services program, were charged with institutionalizing as much of Della's lifelong medical

Della Keats visits with students at the University
of Alaska Fairbanks, 1984.

knowledge as possible. Maniilaq disseminates the information
as books, pamphlets, school lessons, videotapes. Decades after
her death, Maniilaq continued training young people to follow in
Della's footsteps.

Della understood that her healing techniques were not necessarily the old ways of the Iñupiat despite media attention in
her later life advancing that idea. Della knew that just because
something is old doesn't automatically render it good and worth
preserving. In the real world of contrasting cultures, Della dis-
carded the bad to blend what she believed constituted the best of
the old and the new—into the operative present. Today's world
might call that complementary medicine, a blend of western and
alternative health care.

In the final decade of her life, Della was in constant demand.
In 1984, she served as an "elder in residence" for ten weeks at the
University of Alaska Fairbanks. The project brought prominent
Native elders to campus to teach traditional skills and pass on
knowledge to younger generations. In 1983, Della received an

honorary doctor of humane letters in health sciences from the University of Alaska Anchorage. In 1982, Governor Bill Sheffield declared April 24 as Della Keats Day. In 1981, she received the Bella Hammond Award for Volunteer Service, in recognition of her providing health care to so many without pay for so much of her life.

At a retirement banquet in Kotzebue, Della received a jade plaque from Maniilaq Association that read: "In appreciation of Della Keats, tribal doctor, for healing our bodies, minds, and spirits."

Della was not your typical "professor." While teaching at UA-Fairbanks, each day she walked into class wearing a broad smile. She might immediately embrace a student sitting closest to the door. One day, she worked her way to the front of the classroom, exchanging words and belly laughs along the way. Then she took her seat next to the program's director.

"Della, we'd like you to talk a little bit about when you were growing up," he said.

Della began by explaining that there was no school and no church in Noatak on the day she was born in January of 1907. Then she explained the Iñupiaq word, *nalaugmiut*.

"We call it bleached seal skin. No hairs on it," Della said to explain the meaning of *nalaug*. And *miut* means "inhabitants of." So *nalaugmiut* means "inhabitants of bleached seal skin." *Nalaugmiut* is an Iñupiaq word for white people, who arrived in arctic Alaska in increasing numbers during her lifetime.

Della Keats acquired skills from traditional healers while developing her own techniques. With no one available at camp, Della delivered her first baby when she was sixteen.

The summer after Della's birth, a school was established in Noatak. Della, who proved a curious student throughout her life, attended the new school as soon as she was old enough. Her thirst for knowledge and remarkable intelligence led her later to master a physiology book she'd found in Noatak's grade school as she became increasingly interested in healing. She acquired skills from Noatak's traditional healers, too, while developing her own healing techniques. With no one available at camp, Della delivered her first baby when she was just sixteen years old.

Western doctors in Kotzebue felt neither threatened nor superior to Della; for years they worked in cooperation with each other. Della, who never operated on anyone, often referred cases to the medical doctors including broken bones and other injuries and ailments she preferred not to treat or could not treat. She would not continue seeing patients who refused to follow her instructions. "Some peoples always call me back alright. But I point to him, this way," Della said, waving her index finger like an angered schoolmarm. "I say, 'You never do what I tell you. It's better you go to the doctor with the medicine.' I quit helping the person when many times he do that."

One village girl who loved basketball came to Della for help.

"She hurt her ankle," said Della. "She always come back, and I fix, and she still play after I tell her not to play. Three or four times she come back. Still I fix it. Put it back in. But I say, 'This time when you hurt your ankle, don't come back to me. You go to hospital and do what doctors say.'"

Della raised more children than her own three, the result of an unhappy marriage that was arranged at a young age by her family. She remained in Noatak most of her life until moving to Kotzebue in 1963 "when my son get a steady job." Della continued helping people in Kotzebue. Expectant mothers from the surrounding villages often stopped at Della's house for an exam and advice before delivering their babies at the local hospital. Della finally started getting paid when Maniilaq Association established its traditional medicine and tribal doctor program about a decade before Della retired in March 1983.

In the final dozen or so years of her life, Della's fame spread far from her home. She spoke at state and national gatherings of medical professionals. The university named a summer math and science program after Della, a program for Native students seeking health careers.

Yet, to Della's friends, associates, and patients in northwest Alaska, she was always just Della, or Putyuk. In retirement, she remained as busy as ever, traveling extensively to lecture and help people in surrounding villages. For many years, she treated chronic arthritis sufferers, healing and instructing them at Serpentine Hot Springs south of Kotzebue on the Seward Peninsula.

"I love to teach the people," she told an interviewer in the early 1980s for a book published by the Alaska Women's Commission. "I don't want to keep something secret by myself. I'm an old lady now, but from the beginning, I always ask anything that I could learn. Momma used to tell me to teach people what I've done. I tell them not to forget what they learned from their grandparents. It's been so good to me. What the mother use for healing, I always tell them to keep on using it. Not get drugs from hospital.

"Try to be happy all the time, try not to hurt anybody. You can hurt others. It's just like an egg. That you keep, not to crack it, not to drop it, because it's easy to break. If a person comes to you for help, make soft questions to him. That way he'll love you, and you'll love him. We will be happy like in early days. Not unhappy. All my life I wanted to let them know. We need a calm day, a happy day all the time."

Della both witnessed and endured the most serious social problems among fellow Iñupiaq Eskimos, especially the ravages of drug and alcohol abuse.

"Too much, too much," she said.

She sank back into her chair, tightening her shuttered eyes, shaking her head in despair. "That's what I hate. I don't like to see a man with alcohol. These persons that have alcohol at home. I hate it."

Even respected elders, including the esteemed Della Keats, had no immunity from sleepless nights and late-night door-pounding from friends and relatives who'd been drinking.

"Even right now, I scared. I always lock my door. That's the only thing I hate. I never taste alcohol yet in my life. Not even a drop in my life. But they have it too much. They just ruin their brain. That's why people separated right now. Never get together."

Della lamented the rising rates of cancer among the Iñupiat.

"They die from it," she said. "Lots of them. They don't have cancer in old days. Fresh air and eat and never drink. Happy life. Long sleep. Do the work and go to bed early. Only tuberculosis being sickness in early days."

Della figured she knew why so many more fatal diseases have overwhelmed many rural Alaskans, "Different diet," she said. "They mix our food with *nuluagmuit* (white man's) food. We don't drink coffee long time ago and never drink tea. We never eat so much sweets, smoke so much."

Despite the seemingly intractable social problems, with a lifetime of helping and healing in her memory, Della did achieve that elusive state in her own life: happiness. "Worriness is a bad sickness. We're not supposed to have it. We're supposed to be happy all the time. I'm the only one left in my family now. No parents. No brother and sister right now. Just me, still happy. I'm happy. It's good."

Putyuk smiles.

Afterword

Tribal doctor Della Keats left a legacy of healing in Alaska that has continued into the new millennium. Her influence promises to endure for many generations. At age 79 in 1986, Della Putyuk Keats died after a bout with cancer. Even on her death bed she continued to comfort others.

In the decades since Della's death, alternative and natural healing practices have expanded. State-licensed naturopathic doctors now operate thriving practices in Alaska. Acupuncturists, massage therapists, and other alternative health professionals are well-respected. In 2010, a hefty shipment of organic fruits and vegetables was being delivered to northwest Alaska villages from a farm in Washington State. More health professionals practice complementary medicine, a combination of western and alternative techniques. In Kotzebue and in other hub communities, chiropractic care has arrived. Maniilaq's tribal doctor program continues unabated, a testament to a humble woman's drive to heal others throughout her long life.

JOHN CREED is professor of journalism and humanities at the University of Alaska's Chukchi College in Kotzebue, where he has distance taught site-bound students throughout Alaska since 1987. Before joining the UA faculty, he covered business and education for the *Fairbanks Daily News-Miner*.

Ruthie Sampson making seal oil, 1993

22

~ KOTZEBUE ~

Ruthie Sampson gave voice to Iñupiat
Susan B. Andrews and John Creed

RUTHIE TATQAVIN SAMPSON left the world much too soon. Her sudden passing of a stroke in November 2008 at fifty-four shocked everyone who knew and loved northwest Alaska's renowned Iñupiaq scholar and educator.

Throughout her adult life, Ruthie was the unwavering voice moving Iñupiaq language and culture forward in a world awash in English. Today, the Iñupiaq Eskimos of northwest Alaska speak mostly English or village English, a non-standard form of English that mixes some Iñupiaq words. English, not Iñupiaq, has come to rule this part of rural Alaska in recent decades. English is used in the media, on the Internet, at home, at work, in school, in the grocery store—just about everywhere.

Ruthie was trying to stem the tide. She had retired from the Northwest Arctic Borough School District a few years before her death after decades of creating Iñupiaq teaching materials. For years, Ruthie translated proceedings at public meetings for elders over radio station KOTZ and elsewhere.

Even though Ruthie and husband, Luke, had moved upriver from Kotzebue, Ruthie kept advancing the local Native language, teaching Iñupiaq through Chukchi College, Kotzebue's satellite branch of the University of Alaska Fairbanks.

As a Chukchi student herself, Ruthie penned an autobiographic essay for English-composition class as she worked toward her associate of arts degree. Her essay was subsequently published in the anthology, *Authentic Alaska: Voices of Its Native Writers*.

Ruthie described her early life as well as some of the traditional Iñupiaq values instilled in her childhood, including sharing and cooperation.

"As I lived in the village, I also learned that younger people were expected to help elders," she wrote. "We were always to respect and listen to their advice." Ruthie was especially close to her late grandmother, Dora Ballot, "whom I affectionately called *Aana*," which means "grandmother" in Iñupiaq. As a child, she also revered the couple who had raised her own Aana Dora, elders Richard and Fanny Jones.

"I would often pack water and carry wood into their house," she wrote. Then she'd sit "beside a certain window" in their home to enjoy their company. "Only the gentle hissing of a gasoline lantern and an occasional crackling of the wood stove would accompany the silence," wrote Ruthie, who learned Iñupiaq as a child. "Visiting with this old couple did not require that we talk constantly. This is where I learned to appreciate silence."

During her childhood, Ruthie's home village of Selawik, which today has about 800 residents and lies some seventy miles southeast of Kotzebue, did not have a high school, so at age fourteen she moved to Anchorage to attend Dimond High School. "This is when I realized that, although I had attended school for nine years in Selawik, I had never had a chance to study anything about 'the Eskimos.' I was proud that I could speak the Eskimo language, but I was sad that I never learned to Eskimo dance."

Established locally in 1897, the Friends' Church, which remains a dominant force to this day in most northwest villages, had banned traditional Eskimo dancing for decades. Many dances were lost, although some survive and are performed today by local troupes such as the Northern Lights Dancers. According to anthropologist Ernest S. "Tiger" Burch Jr., hardly a single northwest arctic Iñupiaq was a Christian in 1890. Yet, just twenty years later, almost everyone had converted to Christianity, which was spread mainly by Natives converting fellow Natives.

Ruthie Tatqavin Sampson's faith never wavered. At the time of her death, she and Luke were pastors at the Friends' Church in

Shungnak, which, with nearby Kobuk, enjoys the region's strongest presence of spoken Iñupiaq. Ruthie regularly translated Bible passages for church services.

It didn't sit well with Ruthie that she learned more about "the Eskimos" and other Alaska Natives at an Anchorage high school than she ever had growing up in her own Native village. That experience fueled her vision of teaching and celebrating Iñupiaq language and culture in the schools. Ruthie's ambition and keen intelligence could have taken her professional career in many directions. In fact, when she first entered college as a teenager—first at the University of Alaska Fairbanks and then on to Central Washington State College—she was pursuing a degree in social work.

"But I began to doubt my career decision because the social problems seemed so overwhelming and depressing," she wrote. "Although I felt compelled to help my fellow Eskimos, I wanted to work at a job that was fun and interesting."

Back in Kotzebue and working as a disc jockey at KOTZ radio, at nineteen Ruthie met her future husband. She would spend most of the rest of her life in the northwest arctic, although she also lived in Washington state, in many places throughout Alaska, and even in Okinawa, Japan. As a young adult, Ruthie began working with village researchers who were gathering traditional stories before they were lost with the passing of generations of elders. She became fascinated while listening to elders' tapes of their stories and traditional activities. She yearned for young Native students to retain their language, culture, and heritage for generations to come. "I became committed to the idea of transferring the information from our elders to students in the local school system," she wrote.

Ruthie spent the rest of her life publishing a wide array of Iñupiaq teaching materials, including books of stories. For years anyone with a question about language or culture knew Ruthie at the school district would willingly supply generous, immediate, methodical answers. (She also graciously offered to bestow on new arrivals their Iñupiaq names, including our own children.)

Ruthie's commitment to explain Iñupiaq terminology

thoroughly and deeply remained as solid as ice at 60 below. She cared deeply about the integrity of the language wherever used.

Ruthie Sampson

According to Ruthie, Iñupiaq Eskimos share or borrow other words from Yup'ik Eskimos farther south, including the word *kuspuk*, which comes from the Yup'ik word *qaspeq*, "a hooded top garment, often made of calico material." The Iñupiaq word for this same hooded garment is *atikluq*. Then there's the Iñupiaq word for Native food: *niqipiaq*; for dried meat, *paniqtaq*; for dried fish, *paniqtuq*; and for frozen fish, *quaq*.

Ruthie spent years learning, cataloging, and publishing her language for posterity and to buttress her own traditional values. "I tend to think of my commitment to the Eskimo language and culture as a strong, driving force in my life," she wrote. "I am able to work with information provided by the elders. It is the way I feel I can help other Iñupiaq people...helping others was instilled in me as a child."

Ruthie's commitment to explain Iñupiaq terminology thoroughly and deeply remained as solid as ice at 60 below. She cared deeply about the integrity of the language.

A few years before she died, Ruthie (her given name) briefly tried to use the more formal "Ruth." "It's more grown-up sounding now that I've reached middle age," she said with her endearing chuckle, the one that told the world she never took herself too seriously. The attempt to have people call her Ruth didn't work out so well because Ruthie was, and always will be, well, Ruthie. Or Tatqavin.

Ruthie was honored extensively for her work. She received numerous awards, including the 2007 Alaska Association of Bilingual Education President's Award for "her lifetime commitment to documenting, teaching, and writing about Iñupiaq language and culture and her many years of administrative service to the children, parents, and schools of the Northwest Arctic Borough."

Ruthie's family says she was most happy when out in the country, listening to the birds, picking flowers, enjoying nature. She picked berries by the bucketful. She fished at camp with family and friends. She cherished her time in nature but also loved to read. And visit with elders.

In her essay, Ruthie describes how the village cooperates after someone dies, from "local talented carpenters" who build the coffin, to others who dig the grave, who fashion the grave marker, who feed all the helpers. Then, during Christmas week, the family of the deceased reciprocates with gifts to the helpers, ranging from "a simple pair of socks to a beautiful pair of mukluks."

Who would have thought these traditions would be practiced so soon for Ruthie Lee Tatqavin (Ramoth) Sampson?

SUSAN B. ANDREWS lives north of the Arctic Circle in Kotzebue, Alaska, with her husband, John Creed, and family. Susan is professor of journalism and humanities at the Kotzebue branch of the University of Alaska, Chukchi College, where she has taught since 1989. Before coming to Kotzebue, she was anchor and news director at the KTVF-TV, the CBS affiliate in Fairbanks.

JOHN CREED is also professor of journalism and humanities at the University of Alaska's Chukchi College in Kotzebue, where he has distance taught site-bound students throughout Alaska since 1987. Before joining the UA faculty, he covered business and education for the *Fairbanks Daily News-Miner*.

Luke Whitethorn

23

* * * * * * * * * * *

Raising a fisherman in southeast Alaska
Sonja Whitethorn

TODAY I CAN BEST DESCRIBE HIS LANGUAGE as salty. He wears greasy sweats and a baseball cap dotted with fish slime and sea water. He has a four-day growth of beard. Looking happy but weary, he ties up the *Vulcan*, shuts down the engine, throws his sea bag over his shoulder, and heads up the ramp toward home.

Even as a young boy, Luke seemed to need to be near the ocean. I should have known early on that I was raising a fisherman. But no, I thought I was rearing a future yuppie, a four-year-degree person who just happened to enjoy fishing in his early youth.

After all, I grew up on the prairie with parents who expected their children to attend college. We all did. College never was discussed with an "if" but a "when" attitude. I employed this technique with my own children. After Luke's older sister became a teacher, I was lulled into thinking I had a good thing going. Luke, however, had a different agenda.

Should I have known when Luke was two and already had an innate sense of direction? Should I have known when Luke was four and building those small wooden boats, or when he used his birthday money at age five to buy a plastic fishing pole? After that, we would spend day after day at the Petersburg docks, he fishing for herring while I sat reading, drinking coffee, and making sure Luke was wearing a life jacket. Should I have realized that an independent businessman was emerging when Luke kept "losing" clothes at an alarming rate only to discover he was selling them to friends?

By age eight, Luke was spending summers fishing for salmon, halibut and crab with his father, himself a teacher-turned-commercial fisherman. My son was learning to do a man's share of work at a young age, but he rarely complained and never lost interest in what was happening on deck or in the wheelhouse. Even on an infamous halibut trip near Point Hugh when we were caught in a storm with water pouring into the cabin with dishes and pans flying, and with the oil stove smoking, and with Luke and me in survival suits (vomiting), did Luke never think of losing his love of the sea.

"We made it, Mom!"

That was his only comment later.

At about nine, Luke saved his summer earnings and bought a leaky, green wooden river punt with a small motor. That's when the *real* worrying began. At first, we limited Luke to the harbor, navigating from dock to dock. I reminded my son constantly of the importance of oars, life jackets, and a bailing can. Nevertheless, Luke many times "forgot" one, or the other, or all. I found it difficult to let him take those independent steps so young, as I always envisioned the worst-possible consequences. Nonetheless, I sensed I had to take some calculated risks. Something in me knew this was a learning process best begun at a young age.

> **By age eight, Luke was spending summers fishing for salmon, halibut, and crab with his father. My son was learning to do a man's share of work at a young age, without complaint.**

From skiffing in the harbor, Luke soon branched out to Petersburg Creek, a fish pond across the narrows only accessible at high tide. One night Luke had not returned, it was dark, and I was approaching frantic. His father was away fishing somewhere, and, as usual, was missing the current crisis. Did Luke fall in the water and drown? Did his engine quit and he was drifting out to sea? Is he hurt? I wasn't sure if this was a crisis, as kids did get stuck up the creek if they did not remember to leave during high tide. I contacted a friend for advice who knew of a man who sporadically stayed up the creek and who had a phone. Luckily, Ed was home. Looking out the window, he reported seeing four boys in waist-deep water pushing a skiff toward the mouth of the creek.

"They should be home in half an hour," he said with a chuckle.

The creek soon lost its allure. Luke needed to travel farther. He thought it would be great to explore the Stikine River, a 400-mile waterway running from its headwaters in northern British Columbia to its delta just south of Petersburg. I didn't share Luke's enthusiasm. I had heard that even the most experienced boaters could get caught on its sandbars. Why wasn't this kid happy on land?

By age thirteen, Luke had traded in his river punt for a bigger, better skiff. Apparently, the new horizons would keep coming, so I purchased what I still consider a major miracle of inventions—a hand-held VHF radio in a waterproof, floatable bag. Luke now could call for assistance if he needed it. Of course, this hinged on my all-knowing teenager remembering to charge the battery and remembering to take it with him.

Luke's next ocean-bound steps came quickly. Just after he "retired" from his deckhand position for his father at thirteen, Luke obtained a commercial crabbing license. Luke ventured down the narrows with a load of pots. He often spent the night on an old raft with just a piece of clear plastic protecting him from the rain.

In town, Luke would put on his "cool" sunglasses with the hot pink bows and go boat to boat visiting Max, Dennis, Rocky, and Andy—rogue fishermen all, by my estimation, but kind enough to share their knowledge and advice, most of it good, with my son. I might add, though, I did have a little trouble with some of their advice: "You don't really need to refrigerate mayonnaise" and "It's okay to wash potatoes in the crab tank."

Throughout Luke's high-school years, I continually promoted college, stooping so low as to show him the wonderful brochures of colleges by a lake with mountains, with hunting and fishing nearby, with lovely young girls on the beaches. Luke, meanwhile, and by this time a "cool" basketball jock, announced he was taking home economics. The class turned out to be about galley cooking.

Next came a big step. Luke purchased a "real" fishing boat, the *Runnin' Rebel*. All of both Luke's and my time and along with a large share of my retirement money went toward making this old wooden boat safer and more seaworthy. So, at sixteen, Luke became Petersburg's youngest skipper. He employed an eighteen-year-old deckhand. Now, Luke was not only responsible for his own young life but for someone else almost as young. I tried to help. Much to Luke's acute embarrassment, I inspected the cabin of his boat weekly, emptying his cooler into a garbage bag. Luke would be on the deck yelling, "Everything in there is just fine!" Oh sure, raw hamburger floating in pink-tinged melted ice water along with butter and cheese, and no one was sure how long ago the ice had melted. Just fine.

I remember this as the summer that Luke, while crabbing, rescued two young men from a remote beach near Juneau. The men told my son they'd fallen asleep and run their dad's cabin cruiser forty feet up onto the beach. Luke had notified the U.S. Coast Guard and given them a lift into town, and then helped them find a room for the night. The pair said they were delivering the guns they had with them to Ketchikan for their father. Our family was notified a month later that the boat had been stolen and that the men went on to commit armed robbery in Ketchikan. Time has passed. At this writing, Luke owns a newer, better boat. Ever serious about his career, Luke works hard and manages his money well.

"I'd be fishing if I didn't make a dime, just because I love it," he has told me countless times.

Luke has been attending the "college of the sea" for many years, a process so gradual that his own mother didn't see it clearly, guided by a more knowing hand than mine. So what if it isn't "my son the doctor" or "my son the lawyer." My son is a successful fisherman who loves his work.

Who could ask for more?

Afterword

After the author penned this piece about her fisherman son in the mid-1990s, Luke's fishing career expanded. In 2010, he had an even "bigger, better" boat and seines for salmon with a four-man crew. He also crabs and fishes for halibut. Luke married a local girl, Mandie, and the young couple has three boys. Mandie is co-owner of a pizza restaurant.

SONJA JEAN WHITETHORN, born in 1948, lives in Petersburg in southeast Alaska and spends part of each winter in Thousand Palms, California. She has a son who fishes and a daughter who is an English teacher. A retired registered nurse and a commercial halibut fisherman, Sonja finds kinship with her grandmother who homesteaded alone near the Black Hills of South Dakota, living in a sod shanty. The best thing about rural Alaska, she says, is "the relaxed lifestyle, the willingness of people to help one another in times of need, and the awesome beauty."

A sled dog musher's-eye view

＊

RECREATION

THE IMAGE OF NATURE in the national consciousness over the past one-hundred years has fallen away from the concept of nature as "a site of hard and fruitful work" to one of "recreational challenge, aesthetic inspiration, and spiritual solace," Jerediah Purdy wrote in *The American Prospect* magazine.

"America is the country of pristine nature and rugged outdoor enthusiasts, home to The North Face, Patagonia, ubiquitous hiking boots, and the Nature Store, with its upscale bestiary of wild things," explains Purdy. "This is John Muir's America," he writes, referring to the Scottish-born naturalist whose writings helped popularize the idea of directly experiencing America's natural heritage and protecting it.

Visitors from all over the world visit Alaska every year, often assuming that the people living among the mountains, glaciers, and rivers in rural Alaska exist almost incidentally to Alaska's natural grandeur. Many visitors regard Alaska as more of a vast, "unspoiled" wilderness playground than a place where people still live off the land.

"Kayaking and rafting are fine on vacation," said one rural Alaskan. "But try carrying your family's meat supply for the winter in your (non-motorized) rubber raft and see how far you get."

It sometimes shocks visiting urban-dwellers to learn that rural Alaskans travel around "roadless" areas on snowmobiles and four-wheelers and in boats with big motors pushing them up and down river systems and along the coast. To this, a rural Alaskan might respond: "This is where we live. The water is our highway, frozen in winter and liquid in summer. Trails are our highways, too. In rural Alaska we can't travel on interstate highways because we don't have any, and most of the time there's no traditional road at all."

In this section, readers hear from rural Alaskans at play, although their pursuits do not always fall into what most folks consider pure "recreation." It's more a "way of life." For example, Robert Andrews, recreational dog musher and retired school-teacher and principal, describes how dog mushers get along in an unlikely location—rainy and mild southeast Alaska. Iva Baker, in her story about maintaining a competitive Iditarod sled-dog team, shows us that a recreational activity can be a full-time pursuit. Kathryn Lenniger shows us that horses play a role in modern-day Alaska life.

Rural Alaskans still marvel at the astonishing natural beauty around them, whether "working" or "playing."

The snow tends to be heavy and wet in Southeast,
not the best conditions for dog mushing.

24

* * * * * * * * * * *

~ HAINES ~

And they call this mushing
Robert Andrews

FOR SOME, THE THOUGHT OF MUSHING in Alaska conjures a serene scene of cruising down wilderness trails amid gently falling snow. For others, forging through a raging blizzard at 30 degrees below zero constitutes the reality of real Alaska dog driving. Most folks, however, including mushers, have no clue about a small, dedicated group of dog drivers in southeast Alaska who pursue the state's official sport under routinely appalling conditions. While mushing invariably elicits images of dedication and hard work, mushing in southeast Alaska, on the other hand, lends a whole new meaning to those terms.

The Alexander Archipelago, better known to most Alaskans as the "Panhandle" or simply "Southeast," includes scattered islands surrounded by headlands jutting from the coastline. About 73% of the region is within the Tongass National Forest, North America's largest rainforest. Far milder temperatures prevail throughout Southeast compared to the rest of the state, with winter temperatures routinely flip-flopping from moderately cold to well above freezing.

Despite, shall we say, less than perfect conditions, Southeast hosts an assortment of mushers living as far south as Petersburg and as far north as Skagway and Haines. While each participant carries a unique approach to the sport, all find inherent difficulties. To the three basic paces of walking, trotting, and loping, we die-hard mushers in Southeast add the dog paddle.

Ex-Petersburg resident Deb Boettcher hesitates to call herself a musher, although she was considered to be the leading musher in Petersburg. Perhaps Boettcher's frustration with a maximum of just one month of favorable conditions there explains her self-imposed limit of two dogs and a subsequent move. She spins the tale of a would-be musher who purchased land on nearby Kuiu Island for a dog-training site, and then to his surprise, finds that the island is less snowy than his own hometown hundreds of miles south in Washington State. After several frustrating winters in Petersburg, Boettcher decides to relocate to Skagway, where she occasionally borrows a few dogs to cruise in the White Pass area high above town.

Another Skagway dog-driver, John Kourda, came from Venetie, an Athabascan village in northern interior Alaska, where mushing forms the core of winter's existence for many. Kourda used to head out on the trail from his front yard, but in Skagway, he finds the long drive to the nearest snow both discouraging and time-consuming. He estimates a normal two-hour dog run takes five or six hours including the preparation, loading, unloading and travel—effectively slashing the number of trips—and the amount of training—that Kourda allows himself. In Skagway, most homes have small lots, which discourage the keeping of dog teams. So Kourda must keep his own team several miles away on a borrowed site.

Besides the long trip to the "mushing grounds," Kourda also laments the widely differing conditions between his own dog yard and the trail. His motto? "Dress for mess." A dedicated Kourda endures the often-rainy conditions in Skagway stacked against the snow and cold of his mushing destination. A normal run might find him leaving home decked out in rain gear and rubber boots, but once in the pass, he changes into a snowsuit and mukluks.

Other Southeast mushers discuss different, if equally vexing, problems of rainforest mushing. Gail Gilbert, a veteran of the Haines mushing scene, started out with a single sled dog until her kids left for college. Finding Southeast's lack of heavy snowfall a major concern, Gilbert too often must break trail only to find herself sharing it with an abundance of moose that can be ornery in a confined area. Few things are more unnerving than arriving with a group of undisciplined dogs who create a harrowing stand-off with some massive moose who will not be intimidated.

Noticing the encroachment of civilization around Haines over the years, Gilbert sketches the scene of once-untouched logging roads now being plowed farther into the forest each year. She consequently finds encounters with unyielding animals on the trail just slightly more dangerous than the rash of snowmachines and pickup trucks that now ramble through the back country, often at high speeds.

Dan Turner is Haines's hopeful contender in the Yukon Quest, an international sled-dog race between Alaska and the Yukon Territory. Turner has been going to the dogs since purchasing a team of geriatric Siberians years ago. Turner feels that for peak performance, his dogs need training in colder weather to acclimate them to racing conditions. To train effectively for the Quest, Turner found it necessary to rent a cabin on Dezedeash Lake farther north in Canada's Yukon Territory. Training there in temperatures of 50 below zero while temporarily escaping the drip, drip, drip of his Southeast environs, Turner explained that Haines's mild temperatures and lack of snow would have limited him to cart-training rather than sled-training until race time in February. One year, Turner did not safely venture onto the nearby marsh until February 28. Additionally, he points out that training in Southeast, with its dearth of teams, leaves his dogs wondering what to do when meeting or passing another team during the Quest. Turner's strongest grievance as a Southeast musher, however, is the wet—wet dogs, wet dog lot, wet straw, wet training. Wet, wet, wet.

"Haines is the only place in the world a guy has to put Desenex on his dogs. They get fungus and their hair falls out," Turner said with a chuckle.

Turner laments the difficulties of rounding up the necessary gear, food and advice locally, considering the nearest bona-fide mushing community, Whitehorse, requires a five-hour drive north across an international boundary.

Not every dog works out, and with limited demand in the

area for sled dogs, Turner goes through his list of remaining friends rather quickly when seeking homes for his dog-lot misfits. Turner's friends are learning that free sled dogs carry the same stigma as a free used car.

Jim Stanford, another all-wet Haines musher, made his entry into the sport through the back door, shall we say, when his son discovered that girls fascinated him far more than soggy dogs. So Papa inherited his teenager's team of elderly Siberians, the same ones once owned by his good friend, Dan Turner. After a series of upgrades, Stanford—whom I remember proclaiming loudly that he *never* would own more than six dogs—has kept a howling kennel of as many as eighteen. Stanford found the lack of local mushing infrastructure a problem. Haines, a decidedly snowmachine town, doesn't offer a support circle for mushers. As a result, mushing becomes a guess-and-go proposition, which is the case throughout Southeast.

While Stanford views the slush and deep snow of Southeast as good training for tough races, he does admit to being hampered by open rivers. Unlike the north, where rivers become frozen winter highways, Southeast mushers travel only one side or the other. Stanford and Turner also found foot problems to be common, the warmth combined with the pervasive dampness being the source of many cut pads.

Like John Kourda, Deborah Bicknell of Juneau laments the lack of room for her team, which she has kenneled some three miles from home. With training limited to only seven miles of dirt road that she shared with motor vehicles, Bicknell has prepared for races at her training camp in Tagish, a tiny settlement in Canada's Yukon Territory. But Bicknell works in Juneau. To train dogs, she endures a six-hour ferry trip to Skagway, and then a 100-mile drive to Tagish, where she runs her dogs for three days before calling on help from a dog-sitter as she again drives south and catches up on sleep on the return ferry to Juneau. There, the exhausted musher puts in a few days at work before repeating the process.

Part of a mushing family since 1956, Bicknell stayed away from the sport while raising her children, but she discovered she had more time once they left for college, just like Gail Gilbert from

Haines. Bicknell's father's appearance at her door with eleven healthy huskies renewed the urge to compete, and it proved only a few short steps from that welcome gift to today's whirlwind pursuit.

Unique among Southeast mushers, Mark Kissel, a dog-driven guy since 1992, never has taken his dogs out of Juneau. When Kissel picked up a few dogs for skijoring (a Norwegian word meaning "ski-driving," where cross-country skiers use a dog as a draft animal), he had no idea that come spring he would find his body a mass of bruises from knees to armpits. "I needed something I could jump from when I saw a tree coming," says Kissel. So he upgraded to a sled. When I first met Kissel, his method of dealing with dogs in a suburban area exuded creativity. Upon my entering his dog yard and hearing his team clearing their throats instead of barking, Kissel explained that these dogs had come from a musher near Anchorage who had their vocal cords cut to turn the normally noisy bunch into better neighbors.

Kissel admits to frustration with the rain and the occasional snowless winter, but he makes the best of a difficult situation by limiting himself to four dogs and the use of a dog cart. Visitors to Kissel's neighborhood regularly see his son driving this dog-powered vehicle delivering newspapers.

Judy Cooper, a retired state employee, felt she could improve her showing on cross-country ski trips by adding some dog power for skijoring. This led to a small team and, ultimately, to her current kennel of more than twenty dogs. Cooper justified her eventual decision to move to Fairbanks by explaining the futility of keeping a team in urban Juneau. Residential zoning laws require kennel placement 300 feet from any dwelling. While few places in Juneau meet such requirements, the Mendenhall Flats adjoining the busy Juneau International Airport provides a temporary if less than perfect location given the roar of jets, the never-ending din of float planes, and the summer-long whup, whup, whup of the local helicopter fleet ceaselessly hauling loads of tourists. The flats, one of the few areas near town for dog-walking, sees a constant parade of pets that arouse the tethered sled dogs into an uproar and triggering calls about "that noisy dog team." Add to this Juneau's monsoon rainfall and you have very wet dogs wallowing in thick glacial silt soup and crawling into dog houses filled with soggy straw—perfect reasons for a move north.

In 1992, the Haines mushers sponsored what we all hoped would be a spectacular racing event. Haines's location on the historic Dalton Trail had us setting into motion the first Dalton Trail 30 sled-dog race. To lure our Canadian counterparts into our mushing no-man's-land, our race featured a sizeable purse and a scenic thirty-mile trail over many ribboning channels of the Chilkat River, along old logging roads, up narrow switchbacks and along the ridge of the spectacular Sunshine Mountain.

Preparations proceeded beautifully with wide-ranging community support. With a challenging trail readied, the week before the race found the fruit of our efforts deteriorating into Southeast soup. Awakening to the sounds of dripping rain and howling gale-force winds, we could see our race deteriorating before our eyes. Huge snow berms became nothing more than insignificant moguls. Ice bridges vanished as we watched, transforming into running water. Slip and slide became swash, slosh, and slog.

With only days remaining before the race, cancellation became impossible, as many of our visitors didn't even have phones. In the famous words of the Ringling Brothers, "The show must go on." Would this also become a circus?

Mother Nature offered a Southeast surprise. Race day dawned cold enough to solidify our slush. At this point, calling our race the "Haines Ice Classic" would have made more sense.

Then, Mother Nature offered a Southeast surprise. Race day dawned clear and cold enough to solidify our slush. At this point, calling our race the "Haines Ice Classic" would have made more sense. Sleds, careening over hazardous ice—followed by the occasional plunge into shallow, open water—together with the painstaking climb up the steep mountain with its roller-coaster plunge down the other side certainly left the competitors each with their own impression of mushing Southeast.

That night's banquet saw happy faces relating tales of the day. Talk ran from the difficulties in coaxing dogs through open water to the fears of heart attacks while trying to run up a 3,500-foot mountain. Despite the party atmosphere, the Dalton Trail 30 made both its debut and finale in the same year.

A more recent winter race was the Skagway-sponsored Trail of 98, a three-day, 150-mile run from Skagway to Whitehorse, Yukon. Again, the Southeast weather dominated the activities. For those unfamiliar with Southeast geography, Skagway, a mere fourteen miles from Haines by ferry, is a 350-mile drive if you take the long way by road. Even the lack of snow at the starting line would have been a welcome sight to Jim Stanford as he stood on deck of the Alaska ferry, the bucking ship unable to dock in the high winds.

Never a quitter, though, Stanford, armed with a double-dose of determination, returned to Haines, disembarked, and began the long drive around to catch up with the race. Arriving with the race already in its second day disqualified him from the competition, but Stanford, ever in love with this amazing sport, ran the remaining two days for the enjoyment and camaraderie. For his efforts, Stanford earned the race's Sportsmanship Trophy as well as a place in the record book.

We Southeast mushers need a variety of techniques just to survive, for we encounter monumental difficulties. So, why do Southeast folks even consider such a sport? While no Southeast dog-driver would use words like "addiction" or "hooked," all admit to the possibility of a slight mental imbalance. Deborah Bicknell, self-proclaimed workaholic, finds dogs an escape. John Kourda simply says, "Everyone needs a hobby." Jim Stanford says he has always been a musher, he just didn't know it. Dan Turner explains his dependence, which might speak for us all around here, by saying, "Maybe it's because it's kinda' special in Southeast."

ROBERT A. ANDREWS, born in 1945, lives in Hollis, a small community on Prince of Wales Island in southeast Alaska. For many years, he and his wife Margaret, both educators, raised their own meat and most vegetables on a forty-five-acre homestead in the Chilkat Valley north of Haines. The couple raised two boys and dozens of foster kids. Robert worked for more than thirty years as a schoolteacher and principal, mostly in small rural Alaska schools. In retirement, Robert hopes to explore Australia and New Zealand and write children's books and write "a novel or two." In Hollis, he hunts deer and other game, fishes for salmon and red snapper, gardens, and gathers greens and berries. "We're hunters and gatherers again," he said.

John Baker on his four-wheeler

25

. . . .

~ KOTZEBUE ~

Maintaining an Iditarod team
Iva Baker

IN JUNE 1998, OUR FAMILY TRAVELED for the first time to our new summer camp at Sivulliqsi to train our forty dogs for the Iditarod Trail Sled Dog Race. The care and training for three to four dozen sled dogs requires much time, patience, knowledge, and equipment as well as supplies, whether training our dogs at Sivulliqsi, a former experimental farm about seventy-five miles east of Kotzebue, or during the winter months in Kotzebue.

It takes a huge commitment to compete in the Iditarod, known as "The Last Great Race on Earth," which runs approximately 1,161 miles each year from Anchorage to Nome. Our family works hard to keep an Iditarod team that is strong, healthy, and competitive. As I write this, our kennel includes pups less than twelve months old and yearlings one to two years old. All these huskies love to eat. In Kotzebue, we have a four- by five-foot, corrugated—and smelly!—red shed where we cook dog food. We built a "grinder house" where we grind up fish and various meats to make dog food. In Kotzebue, we also operate a walk-in freezer to preserve fish, meats, seal oil, and muktuk to nourish our dogs.

We must feed the dogs every day. This takes at least an hour. To feed twelve dogs one meal requires a five-gallon bucket of water and four large arctic sheefish or salmon, guts and all. We usually let the fish boil for about forty-five minutes, then let it all stand for about an hour. Once cool, we stir the "brew" with a wooden stick to break up the fish. Three-pound coffee cans serve as the dog "dishes." For each dog, we add one cup of commercial dog food, one cup of fish, and one cup of broth from the boiled fish for a delicious, nutritious meal. During the cold winter months, we add one or two cups of seal oil for extra nutrients and flavor.

When I first made homemade dog food for our Iditarod team, I was naive, for I never had cooked dog food before in my life. I since have improved my skills. I watched my husband John chop fish, fill buckets with water, and measure seal oil, explaining as he went along how long to cook the fish, how long to let the fish cool off, and when to add the seal oil. Today, I feel as if I can make a healthy, hearty serving almost every time.

We must feed the dogs every day. To feed twelve dogs one meal requires a five-gallon bucket of water and four large arctic sheefish or salmon, guts and all.

For the cooking pot, we use a fifty-five-gallon drum that is cut in half. We clean it regularly with pressurized hot water; we wouldn't want the dogs eating unsanitary food, for both viral and bacterial infections can spread fast through a kennel of dogs living close to each other.

When we prepare for a training run, first we water the dogs, and then we hitch them up and run them for five to ten miles. During the fall, the dogs typically run that distance every other day, but sometimes every day, depending on their conditioning regimen. During the summer, we hitch up a team of ten dogs to the front of our four-wheeler using a three-eighths-inch rope about fifty feet long called the "towline," which is the centerline fastened to a four-wheeler or sled to which the dogs are hitched up.

The dogs closest to the sled or four-wheeler are called "wheel" dogs, and in our training the "tugline" measures about fifty-five inches long. (Other mushers' tugline measurements might vary.) A tugline, or "tug," runs from the harness to the towline. The dogs between the leaders and wheel dogs are spaced about forty inches apart, and the leaders' tugs span about thirty inches long.

A "neckline" runs from one leader to another leader, standing side by side in the front of the team. The double neckline is approximately twelve inches long.

Harnessing a dog to the towline takes practice. John and I use a collared-neck harness. Harnessing sled dogs is like putting a jacket on for a child. You put the padded collar neck on, then slip the legs through. When preparing for a run, mushers almost always hitch up their leaders first. This keeps the dogs steady and in line, and you don't have to worry so much about the dogs getting tangled up or starting a fight.

Where we live, mushers put "dog jackets" around their canine athletes' midsections to protect them from frostbite when temperatures dip under 20 degrees below zero. Dog booties, those little polyester mittens with no thumbs that are fastened with strong Velcro, help protect the dogs' feet from jagged ice and "snowballs" that build up on their pads and between their toes, causing splits and cuts. We always clean our dogs' paws before putting on their booties.

We constantly work to keep our dogs healthy. All our sled dogs are vaccinated against certain diseases and are wormed every year. If a flu or bad cold runs through our dog lot, however, we simply allow it to run its course because usually there is nothing we can do about it.

We also take other health precautions around the dogs, such as wearing rubber gloves, coveralls, boots, and regular knitted gloves. When we are done feeding the dogs, running the dogs, and cleaning up their poop, we store our work clothes in a designated area to help prevent germs from spreading around the house. To be candid, sometimes our clothing really stinks from working so closely with so many dogs—that's another reason to quarantine our work clothes.

In the winter when it gets cold, 30 below or lower, my husband and I place straw in our dogs' little houses. At these extreme temperatures, we also keep the dogs in a dog barn that can fit up to twenty dogs. This structure is only eight feet by ten feet, dimensions that make it small enough for the dogs to conserve their body heat. Each dog has a box with straw that is warmed with the dogs' body heat. We haven't had any dogs die, thank goodness; we never keep dogs in the "barn" for more than eight hours because of possible suffocation.

Maintaining a dog team takes a lot of time and effort to raise, feed, and train. You also have to clean up poop around the yard. Our husky dogs are playful, huggable, fluffy, cute animals you can't resist petting, and as the saying goes, dogs are a person's "best friend."

IVA MAY BAKER, an Iñupiaq born in 1970, has two Iñupiaq names— Nunuraq and Ilaguq. She is married to John K. Baker, a well-known top competitor in the Iditarod Trail Sled Dog Race, in which he is a perennial top-tier contender. They have two children and live in Kotzebue in northwest Alaska. She says the best thing about living in rural Alaska is that "less than twenty miles out of Kotzebue, you can be in the country where there is quietness." She believes in continuing to learn and grow because "with God, all things are possible."

Horses have been a major
part of Kathy Lenniger's life.

26

* * * * * * * * * *

~ NENANA ~

A second chance
Kathryn Lenniger

MY SMALL CHILDREN FINALLY had fallen asleep on a late August night, and there was a moment of tranquility before a startling, violent sound, accompanied by deep thuds, pierced the air outside our cabin. Looking through the bedroom window into the twilight, I saw my beloved horse, Treetop, his head extended downward as he frantically searched the ground.

He was gasping for air.

I raced to the corral and threw open the gate as Treetop fell repeatedly into the wall of his stall, his nostrils flaring. I screamed his name. He staggered toward me, wide-eyed and desperate. Then his great body collapsed in the dirt. Panic-stricken, I attached Treetop's lead line to his halter and jerked him, shakily, to his feet. Then I sprinted for the telephone.

The veterinarian lived more than an hour away, and as I pleaded with him to hurry, my husband walked in from the corral.

"Tell him to stay home," he said. "Treetop is dead."

Doug's words hit so hard that I actually felt I had received blows. That this impressive animal never again would run to greet me seemed impossible. Grief and anger at Treetop's sudden demise remained a long time, his empty, silent corral a daily reminder.

Like many young girls, as a child I had dreamed of having a horse of my own. Equine photos and books had filled my room.

My imagination rode daily as we leaped over fences and galloped down dusty country roads, but a real horse never did appear in my childhood suburban home. As an adult, I rode whenever I could, but my lifestyle couldn't accommodate the care of a large animal. Nevertheless, the shock of my fortieth birthday brought home the realization that only I could fulfill the dreams of a youth slipping away.

Treetop, a twelve-year-old bay gelding, came to me after being selected by an equestrian friend at an auction. As she backed Treetop from her horse trailer to his new corral at my home, the animal's well-defined muscles danced under the blue blanket. Aptly named at a towering sixteen hands high, Treetop turned a massive head, framed with inquisitive brown eyes, to consider his fate.

Awkwardly, we learned about each other. Testing his new owner, Treetop would gallop down the dirt road in front of our cabin at full speed while I clung to the saddle, terrified. This had not been part of my fantasy.

Determination, provoked by mutual need, fueled our attempts at friendship. I brushed Treetop's glossy coat daily while bribing him with carrots. Turning in circles, we mastered the lunge line. The supreme equestrian test came one day a year later, as I carefully climbed onto Treetop's back without a saddle. My fingers entwined in his thick black mane. Responding to the pressure of my legs, he surged forward into the forest. I moved rhythmically with his cadence, trusting the tremendous force beneath me, a young girl again. After that day, Treetop nickered softly whenever I came near.

This family friend's death came much too soon.

The expense of a new horse made a replacement unlikely. Nevertheless, about nine months later, a call came with the offer of a condemned horse as potential food for my hungry sled dogs. A veterinarian, I was told, upon examining this emaciated and reportedly toothless animal, had declared him to be in such poor condition that, at the advanced age of thirty-five, rehabilitation was impossible. As a practical person, I accepted the offer, if reluctantly.

The next day, a small form backed unsteadily out of a horse trailer in my driveway. At fourteen hands high, there stood a filthy, matted hide stretched over not much more than the skeleton of a male horse. Shocked, my finger slipped easily between this forlorn creature's ribs. Vertebrae, clearly outlined in a row down his back, marched between sharply protruding hipbones. Liquid feces stained the scrawny hairs of a tail, and ridges twisted his split hooves. Even the pungent horse aroma I love had fled this poor beast. Yet, these eyes, brown and surprisingly clear, looked expectantly at me.

There stood a filthy, matted hide stretched over not much more than the skeleton of a male horse. Shocked, I slipped my finger easily between this forlorn creature's ribs.

Too thin to warrant the effort of slaughter, our new arrival's fate became the subject of an internal debate. I felt confused. The old fellow walked casually into Treetop's corral, lowering his head to inspect the bare ground. With uncertainty, I gave him leftover hay, afraid that without teeth the rough silage might lodge in his throat.

Without hesitation, however, this new horse chewed and swallowed the entire pile! Amazed, I offered more hay, and then a bucket of oats, which disappeared just as quickly.

Each succeeding morning, I looked over at the corral, expecting to see a prone form. Instead, our new arrival stood chewing at the hayrack.

My son, with youthful optimism, named the old boy Fireball.

Gradually Fireball's diarrhea disappeared and his ribs slipped slowly behind ever-thickening flesh. He stood perfectly still, with closed eyes, when I brushed out the dirt and combed his sparse, black mane. Within six weeks Fireball had gained 300 pounds. One day, after inspecting his expanded girth, I grabbed Treetop's old saddle from the barn. Gently placing it on Fireball's back, I tightened up the cinch after adding several notches and cautiously climbed on. Fireball walked toward the road, then burst comfortably into a trot. A second veterinarian offered a markedly different opinion from the first vet's prediction of imminent death.

"This horse has all his teeth and I'd say he's about twenty-three years old," I was told. "He appears quite healthy."

When Fireball heard that, he stopped chewing, turned, met my eyes, and gave me what I swear was a wink.

By the time winter arrived, Fireball's enthusiasm for eating had added weight until his dark coat grew thick and dappled. His back remained unusually level because of previous emaciation, the veterinarian had explained, as normal weight curves the spinal cord over the passage of time. Fireball's hooves took an entire year to grow out straight and hard. To my surprise, the vet's next visit pronounced our new family member to be in ideal physical condition.

Like Treetop, Fireball ties out calmly, an uncommon trait with equines, trimming the lawn and wild grasses from the length of his tether. He lacks the impressive form of his predecessor, but my children love to feel their youthful legs wrapped around a horse's broad back while Fireball greets each new day with a high-pitched whinny.

KATHRYN ANN LENNIGER, born in 1949, moved to Fairbanks in recent years after living in Nenana in interior Alaska for twenty-six years. She describes her ethnicity as "part Cherokee, part mystery," having been adopted. A mother of two, Lenniger is a professional dog musher and owner-operator of Sled Dog Adventures, a Fairbanks company that markets dogsled rides, tours, and mushing instruction. She also has wrangled horses, run a wilderness lodge, and creates artwork and signs. She holds a bachelor of arts degree in psychology with significant fine arts coursework. Living in rural Alaska, she says she has learned "tolerance, acceptance, and the meaning of community."

Historical photo of 300-pound halibut caught in Juneau, 1910

✳

CULTURE

OUTSIDE ALASKA, "RURAL" IS EASY to visualize. It conjures images of "amber waves of grain" on the Great Plains. It invokes an idyllic scene in, say, Rocky Mountain ranch country where cattle graze under big blue open skies. Or in Vermont, with its tranquil green fields, stately hardwoods and evergreens, blood-red barns, pure-white churches with that single stately spire stabbing the sky amid a backdrop of flaming fall foliage and gently rolling hills. In effect, rural usually means "farm country," interspersed with woodlands.

Some parts of Alaska resemble the rest of the country's classic rural image. Take the Matanuska-Susitna Valley, also called the Mat-Su, just north of Anchorage in southcentral Alaska. That's where a group of "colonists" from the Midwest, as part of President Franklin D. Roosevelt's New Deal, ventured into the wide valley in 1935 to carve traditional working farms out of the wilderness.

Today, stunning snow-capped mountain peaks of the Alaska Range frame the magnificent Mat-Su's gently rolling farm country. The 1930s farming families who stayed each began with about forty acres of land. They created a traditional rural way of life around the newly founded town of Palmer. Much of this original ground is where almost three-quarters of Alaska's homegrown agricultural products come from today. Nevertheless, the classically rural Mat-Su Valley, along with the miniscule agricultural lands that cluster around communities served by the state's relatively modest road system, is the exception rather than the rule.

For most Alaskans, "rural" or "bush" does not bring farming or agriculture to mind.

As Alaskans know, traditional roads that connect to the outside world exist only in one corner of the state—between Anchorage and Fairbanks and on the Kenai Peninsula and over to Tok and down to Valdez, the trans-Alaska pipeline's southern terminus. In southeast Alaska, imposing, rugged, glacier-draped mountain systems block road access to the outside world. The Alaska Marine Highway, a ferry system, transports passengers and motor vehicles among some twenty-eight towns as well as to British Columbia and as far south as Bellingham, Washington.

Out on the Aleutian Islands, a road never will connect these remote, far-flung, wind-battered islands like a highway connects the Florida Keys to the mainland.

Alaska remains mostly roadless. That unusual fact fosters a unique way of life that this final group of writers explores amid today's multi-connected modern world.

Schoolteacher Wilma Payne shares a common cultural experience of many rural Alaskans: shipping goods home from Alaska's cities and strapping and/or Duct Tape's role in that endeavor. Gina M. Pope tells us why VHF radio still works so well as a way for a people with a strong oral tradition to keep in touch. Many Alaskans have bizarre stories about how they spent their first few winters in Alaska. One could say Terry Wilson lived more like a groundhog than a human being in his first Alaska home. Lucy Daniels explores cultural differences that "village" English reveals with its heavy influence from Alaska Native languages.

Al Bowling chronicles cultural changes he witnessed in the tiny village of Deering in northwest Alaska after satellite television arrived. Finally, Katie Cruthers ends this anthology with an insightful essay on the enduring Iñupiaq idiom: *Adii!* This expression bears numerous meanings, depending on the context and the speaker's inflection.

Strapping tape used as makeshift gaiters to
protect boots and pants bottoms

27

• • • • • • • • • • • •

~ MCGRATH ~

Don't leave home without strapping tape
Wilma C. Payne

WHEN WE MOVED INTO OUR FIRST HOME in rural Alaska, fresh from the Lower 48, I was surprised to find Duct Tape or strapping tape, adorning nearly every visible surface.

The old kitchen chairs wobbled, their faded red plastic backs taped to aluminum frames. A mirror reclined against the bedroom wall, steadied with strapping tape. The doorknob to the pantry dangled on an ingenious harness made from crossed strips of Duct Tape, doubled and wrapped around it. The same sticky stuff mended the rip in the upholstery of the couch and a crack in the living room window.

The hem of the drapes had come loose, and—you guessed it—strapping tape rejoined them.

I soon realized that in Alaska, nylon or fiberglass tape is indispensable. When they have strapping tape in their toolbox, first-aid kit, or backpack, folks in the bush are ready for almost any emergency.

Experienced bush residents often carry a roll or two of strapping tape when they travel. Cardboard boxes serve well as luggage, but you don't want your gear scattered from Shageluk to Holy Cross if the bush pilot is less than gentle with your treasures. So, strapping tape serves as latch, lock, and safety strap for all your carefully chosen pieces, from tasteful egg or apple crates, to cartons emblazoned with famous designer names such

Using strapping tape to
reattach a side-view mirror

as Diet Pepsi or Coca-Cola.

My husband—more inventive than I—once fashioned a lovely carrying case for a few power tools while on a short trip to visit family in the Lower 48. He wrapped an empty Oreo cookie case horizontally, vertically, and diagonally with parallel ribbons of tape. On the final two rounds, he left a little slack at the top and wrapped strapping tape tightly around the loose strands, creating a double carrying handle made of the omnipresent strapping tape. I'm sure it was noted with awe by baggage-handlers and ticket agents from Seattle to Durango.

Strapping tape serves as an all-purpose protective covering when you don't have a mailing carton. A case of paper towels, for instance, once came through the mail without a rip or a tear. In all my scrounging that trip, I hadn't found a cardboard box large enough to hold all twenty-four rolls. So, I diligently wrapped layer after layer of strapping tape around the thin plastic covering and affixed an address label to the outer layer. The postal clerk didn't bat an eye, and the whole gob made it home just fine.

Strapping tape serves as an all-purpose protective covering when you don't have a mailing carton. A case of paper towels once came through the mail without a rip or tear.

Strapping tape finds its way onto every shopping list I take to town. How can we possibly use those dozens of rolls? Well, we have to replace the roll in the first-aid kit in case we need quick, tight fasteners for a bandage. Some goes into the snowmachine toolbox for emergency repairs, such as taping broken spark plug wires onto the plugs or replacing the hitch pin for the sled. A roll hangs on a nail in the woodshed for a quick, temporary reinforcement if the splitting maul or ax handle cracks. Tuck one into the diaper bag, too, in case the tape on the baby's disposable diaper rips off during a crucial change.

I've used strapping tape to hold batteries in the radio, to cover the lock socket so the door won't lock behind me when I dash to the woodpile in my nightgown and slippers, to secure the branches of my artificial Christmas tree to the old broomstick I use for a trunk, and to repair the windshield after rolling my brand-new snowmachine off a snowdrift in the front yard.

What else can you use strapping tape for? New uses crop up every day. My daughter's Barbie doll lost her head the other day. I didn't lose mine; I just reached for the strapping tape.

WILMA C. PAYNE, born in 1950, lives in Pueblo, Colorado. A mother of two, she taught for twenty-four years in rural Alaska villages, including Stony River, Nikolai, and McGrath. She holds a master's degree in elementary and secondary education. Of rural Alaska, she says, "It was a good place to raise my children. The village is like an extended family, with plenty of good friends and support."

CB Channel 30

28

~ KOKHANOK ~

What's your call sign?
Gina M. Pope

IN OUR VILLAGE OF KOKHANOK on the shores of Lake Iliamna in southwest Alaska, we primarily use VHF radios to communicate with one another. To some extent, we communicate with other villages by the same method. The VHF, which is on a different frequency than the citizens' band radio, allows us to keep in touch with the local "news" because so many local people use it.

The VHF radio has a range of about forty nautical miles, but it can reach up to ninety miles under ideal circumstances. The radio has about one-hundred channels, but most folks using the VHF "stand by," keeping their radio tuned to a certain channel, in this case channel ten, to have a common channel to reach each other. Some businesses use another channel to cut down on the traffic on channel 10.

Local people also use a hand-held VHF radio with a range of five to fifteen miles. These are handy when traveling and useful to ensure safety. For instance, a person can call back to the village for help if a member of the party is injured and needs assistance. People who are lost and are fortunate enough to have a hand-held VHF can radio back to the village for help.

In Kokhanok, we can pick up conversations in the neighboring villages of Iliamna, Newhalen, Nondalton, Pedro Bay, Iguigig, and Port Alsworth. The drawback, unfortunately, is that while we can hear all these places, we cannot transmit back to all of them. I can speak only with people in the neighboring villages who have high, well-placed antennas for their radios.

News travels faster on the VHF radio than over any other media in our village, including the telephone. Everyone on VHF is able to hear news simultaneously. It is a need we have, being so closely connected by birth and by choice. We know soon when someone passes away. We know who won the dog races at the carnival, who caught the first salmon of year, and how many fish so-and-so caught in their net. By listening in to conversations, we know if the ice is safe, if there are pressure cracks, and what the weather might be.

Of course, some news is taboo on the VHF. For instance, people do not discuss moose shot out of season. Fish and Game officials have VHF radios, too. Out of common courtesy, people do not argue or use profanity on the radio. Some communications can be annoying; for example, if a person "plays" with the radio—disguising his or her voice, whispering, or clicking the microphone button excessively. Such unidentifiable persons are reprimanded quickly by the general listening audience on channel ten: "Quit playing with the radio!"

Some news is taboo on the village VHF radio. For instance, people do not discuss moose shot out of season. Fish and Game officials have VHF radios, too.

Many people have a telephone, but VHF radios hold an important place in our community—a place I would surely miss should the little "talk box" ever become obsolete.

GINA MARIE POPE, born in 1965, leads a mobile life of traveling for work within the Bristol Bay region. She enjoys berry-picking, basket-weaving, and preserving local food in Dillingham. She is a knitter for the Oomingmak Musk Ox Producers Cooperative. A state-certified teacher, Gina holds a master of education degree in early childhood. She works as an early-intervention teacher for the Bristol Bay Area Health Corporation's Infant Learning Program. In addition, she travels to villages in rural Alaska certifying candidates for associate degrees in child development for the Council for Professional Recognition, a national accreditation agency. She holds a calling in the Church of Jesus Christ of Latter Day Saints as a teacher of children in primary grades. Her personal goals include earning a doctorate to address issues of regional sustainability and being a "good person that the younger generation can love and remember."

Terry Wilson with Tutkiksuk, his canine companion

29

~ NOME ~

An Alaska winter under the snow
Terry Wilson

HE STEPPED OFF HIS SNOWMACHINE and scanned the horizon, looked at me, then pulled up his goggles, turning in a full circle to scan the northwest Alaska horizon. I could see an almost fearful look in his eyes.

"This...*this*, is where you live?" he stammered. "I don't see any house."

I had to tell him, twice, "Yes, this is where I live," pointing toward the piece of pipe nearby sticking up out of the snow.

"Thanks much for the ride," I said, gathering my things off his snowmachine.

I was feeling guilty leaving him standing and staring as I trudged up the bank toward my little hole in the snow, the entrance to my pole-and-plastic tent, now totally covered with snow. Maybe I should have taken time to explain. After all, he had been kind enough to give me a ride down the Bering Sea ice from the local college, a kindness that had saved me a good hour's walk. And that trek, at times, could prove dangerous if I were to step into an open lead or crack in the ice or were to become lost in the blinding snow with no landmarks to follow.

I guess I ended up here because I was blessed from a young age with a great spirit of adventure and survivability. I remember the story my parents told me of my birth in Wisconsin, just eighteen days before the bombing of Pearl Harbor in December 1941. I'm told I arrived eight weeks early, looking like a little, gray, wrinkled old man, weighing less than five pounds. I was laid aside as the doctor worked frantically to save my mother's life. I believe that was the first time my angel was on duty. Intent on keeping that angel working overtime, as a child I loved to climb. I loved to sneak to Grandma's house a quarter-mile away unless my dog, Jiggars, dragged me back by my diaper.

I spent my preteen years in an abandoned mining town high in the Colorado Rockies. My brothers and sisters and I often played on an old, three-story gold dredge in our backyard. We explored abandoned cabins, mining mills, and gold mines. My youngest brother and sister always had to tell on the rest of us. My reward for the adventure would be a spanking, plus extra kindling-splitting and coal-carrying duty.

After finishing high school, I didn't do well in college. So, in 1960, a friend and I traveled around the country in my pickup with the idea of working our way to Alaska. But we both got side-tracked by women once back in Colorado. Within a year, I was married and blessed with a fine, red-haired son named Scott.

Alaska still loomed on my mind as we moved to Oregon singing, "We're gonna have fun in '61." While working in an all-night service station in Oregon, I became interested in law-enforcement and joined a local police agency. I had a good background in mountain-climbing and scuba-diving and wanted to specialize in search and rescue. My main duty was patrol with mountain rescue and underwater recovery on a volunteer basis. In March 1964, I was shot in the line of duty, but survived, thanks to my angel. My second son, Timothy, was born a short time later on Friday, the thirteenth of May.

As my sons grew, eventually I left law-enforcement and started teaching scuba-diving and commercial diving, which allowed more time to take my sons hiking, camping, diving, and sailing. They were growing fast and were forging their own adventures into music with their own teenage band. We had become three proficient bachelors for one whole year after a "it-could-never-happen-to-me" divorce.

The old tune "North to Alaska" by Johnny Horton was on constant replay in my mind and could not be turned off no matter how hard I tried. One evening, as the three of us sat at the round table, I blurted out, "Well, Dad's going to Alaska!" I received a silent stare. I could even hear the clock ticking for what seemed a long time. Then came the reply, "Well, Dad, isn't it supposed to be that we grow up and then we leave home, not we grow up and then *you* leave home?" That was in 1981.

Although both sons joined me in Alaska for a while, prior to getting married and having fine sons of their own, they watched that clock's second hand slice through time in another place. Then, one night in 1990, I received a call that my youngest son, Tim, had passed away.

> One evening, as the three of us sat at the table, I blurted out, "Well, Dad's going to Alaska!" Silence. I could even hear the clock ticking for what seemed a long time.

Now, each day that passes since that sad time brings better memories, along with another adventure of working under the ocean, or videotaping a shipwreck of the past or just watching the waves roll up on the beach around Nome. Or, taking the walk home in winter, when I often enjoy watching the soft orange sun slide along the jagged edge of the ice and slip quietly below the horizon, leaving me only with the sound of my footsteps echoing, as if walking down great white marble halls.

This particular day when I got a lift, though, I knew the snowmachiner was still watching as I crawled headfirst into the snow tunnel and disappeared from his sight; I chose not to contemplate what my friend must have been thinking.

I pushed open my door, stood upright in the dim light, and walked to a small homemade round table to light the oil lamp. I stood a moment, looking at my small, sparkling palace. A rusty World War II cot, covered by my orange expedition down sleeping bag, sat on one side of the room. A small, round table filled the center. On the other side a diminutive cast-iron woodstove next to an old weathered cabinet supported my Coleman two-burner camp stove. Nearby was a place to hang my "parky," diving drysuit, and some other diving gear. Below that was a small hole in the ground, which served as a refrigerator in summer, a freezer in winter. The "kitchen" floor was covered with flat stones, the "living room" and "bedroom" floor with boards from part of a ship that had washed up onto the shore of the Bering Sea.

My home was a palace to me, after having spent until the previous January living on board a steel ship frozen in the ice. The vessel had become a dark, dangerous, unbearable place to live after its owners had abandoned it without fuel and discontinued my monthly stipend. I was glad to be off it, as pipes had burst in the night. It had taken on a twenty-five-degree list even while frozen in the ice. My new home under the snow was quiet and peaceful, even when the wind got howling mad and no life moved outside. I had become used to the freezing-cold floor and going to bed wearing my beaver hat. What I had not gotten used to, however, was occasionally waking up with four small cold feet and a warm furry belly resting in the middle of my forehead, but I'm certain that little shrew was as surprised as I was, when he found himself flying across the room.

My life, frankly, had become quite lonely until a wild dog had left a delightful pup for me in a hole in the bank. We became instant friends and constant companions. She answered to "Tukiksuk," which in Eskimo means peace, love, and contentment. She taught me more than I taught her.

I spent time contemplating the different layers of snow I could see through the clear plastic walls of my modest little home, thinking about the people who had lived in tents under the snow during the gold rush in Nome around 1900.

I was not the first to live like this. I thought of Eskimos, who until relatively recently had lived in sod huts, and of how much warmer I could have been with two feet of sod covering my simple abode. I felt out of place because the only Eskimo I knew in the 1980s had a real house, with oil heat, cable television, and electric lights at the flip of a switch. Still, I was filled with pride and humility at the same time about the hardships our ancestors endured. But in my heart, I understand the pride they surely felt, knowing one can be happy with little and can live with Mother Nature as a friend rather than as something to be conquered.

The old adage suddenly took on a entirely new meaning for me: "Have not, want not" could really only mean "Have not, need not."

TERRENCE B. WILSON, born in 1941, lives near Homer in Southcentral Alaska but formerly lived for twenty-three years in Nome. He has raised two boys. He has worked as a commercial diver, underwater welder, and an adjunct instructor in marine safety and photography for the University of Alaska. Terry has been involved in search and rescue operations and has been an emergency medical technician. He has an abiding interest in photography. According to Terry, the greatest things about rural Alaska are the challenges and the "camaraderie of fellow citizens." He looks forward to operating a sail-dive charter so that he may "share Alaska's underwater secrets and history with others."

A fish camp in northwest Alaska

30

* * * * * * * * * * *

Eskimo language affects English
Lucy Nuqarrluk Daniels

MARRYING MY HUSBAND JERRY in December 1982 in-troduced me to a part of Alaska with language variations that were new to me. I had visited the Norton Sound region only once, in 1981 when I attended a Covenant Church conference in Shaktoolik. Jerry and I had met while I was a student at the University of Alaska Fairbanks. We got married in Unalakleet, in the Norton Sound area, where Jerry was an intern under the Reverend Donald Erickson, then the Covenant Church pastor.

I grew up in the Kuskokwim area in the more southern part of the state, speaking Yup'ik exclusively, except to my teachers and their children. I had learned English in elementary school. In my new home in northwest Alaska, however, I noticed that my Iñupiaq and Yup'ik peers spoke almost entirely in English. A num-ber of the older residents either spoke both Iñupiaq and Yup'ik, and also English, or they spoke one of the two Eskimo languages, understood the other, and spoke English as well.

Unalakleet's geographical position as a border town be-tween the Yup'ik area to the south and the Iñupiaq area to the north probably explains this phenomenon. In fact, the name "Unalakleet" is the anglicized version of the Yup'ik *Ungalaqliq,* meaning "one to the south" or, perhaps, "southernmost." My guess is that Unalakleet is "the southernmost" point as far as the Iñupiaq language and race are concerned. It was in Unalakleet where a good friend and I were talking in Yup'ik, when my friend's

Iñupiaq husband informed us, "You can't keep any secrets from me, because I know what you're saying."

In fact, my mother-in-law, Beatrice Daniels, who speaks Yup'ik, can carry on a conversation with an Iñupiaq speaker, although I've never heard her talk in Iñupiaq. Her guest speaks to her in Iñupiaq, and she answers in Yup'ik (or Unaliq, the Norton Sound dialect of Yup'ik) or English. In the Norton Sound area, English had become the main language as the latter half of the 1900s turned into the new millennium.

A Unalakleet woman in her seventies explained that she and her peers were required to speak only English when she was a child in school. They were punished whenever they spoke their own language. Thus, to spare their own children the same abuse and embarrassment, she said, they talked to them in English at home. Their children then grew up speaking the dialect of English that they heard at home, a mixture of the Eskimo languages and English, which reflects Eskimo thought patterns. Perhaps because my peers and I in the lower Kuskokwim area never were forbidden to speak Yup'ik in school, we retained Yup'ik as a first language and still learned English as we progressed in school.

Although one of my teachers occasionally ordered us to speak English, he never punished us for conversing in Eskimo. At the same time, speaking English to anyone other than my teacher felt unnatural. It was embarrassing to perform the annual school Christmas plays, which were delivered entirely in English, especially if we actors had to converse with each other in front of our parents.

When I was a student teacher in a village in 1981, I stayed with a family whose main language was Cup'ik (not Yup'ik, mind you). A two-year-old boy, who spoke only English, interested me. His father spoke only Cup'ik. However, his mother spoke mostly Cup'ik and a little English. His older siblings, ranging in age from about ten to about twenty-two, who spoke both English and Cup'ik, talked to the little boy only in English. When I recounted the story to my friend Steven Jacobson, a linguist who teaches Yup'ik grammar at the UA Fairbanks, he explained that the little boy spoke only English because the other family members spoke to him in English, though they spoke to each other in Cup'ik. The same thing happened in the Norton Sound area. For instance, Jerry's parents conversed in Unaliq but spoke to their children in English, so today they speak mainly English.

Though my peers in the Norton Sound area spoke English almost exclusively, I began to notice how the Eskimo languages of their ancestors had influenced their "village English." In fact, their parents and grandparents had developed handy shortcuts and "handles" for some of the suffixes too cumbersome to translate into English but which give the Eskimo language its subtle shades of meaning that are too important to leave out of the English translation altogether. My peers here in the Norton Sound area had "inherited" these special meanings. I already knew about the "funny" way we, who had grown up speaking Yup'ik, spoke English. Because some of the English sounds are absent in Yup'ik, we simply chose a sound closest to the one we wished to produce in English. In this way, the Eskimo language also influenced the way we spoke English.

From Steven Jacobson, I learned that the following examples of how the Eskimo languages affected English are true of both Central Yup'ik and Iñupiaq. However, I will draw most of the examples from the lower Kuskokwim and Norton Sound areas, where I have lived, and use my knowledge of the lower Kuskokwim dialect of Central Yup'ik, which I speak and studied as a major at the UA Fairbanks.

An example of village English: one summer at fish camp, Jerry walked into our cabin and told me, "Paniuq's got some chicken, arright." Jerry's aunt, Paniuq had fried some chicken and was offering us some. My high school English teacher told me that "arright" was wrong and that "all right" is right, but in this case, "all right" is definitely all wrong, because the Norton Sound Eskimos have adopted the word "arright" to translate a suffix that's often used in Eskimo but is missing in English.

A good friend, who served as a missionary with her husband in an Alaska Indian village, once told me that the village children would ask, "Where's my other-side glove?" when about to venture out into a cold winter day. I've also heard my mother-in-law ask a grandchild, "Where's your one-side shoe?"

In my dialect of Yup'ik, we use a word when referring to one of a pair—such as socks, shoes, gloves, mittens. According to the *Yup'ik Eskimo Dictionary*, this word, *inglu,* can mean "other one of a pair; enemy, rival, opponent." When I lose a sock, I can ask, "*Suukiima inglua nauwa?*" The translation as "Where is my other sock?" suffices in English, but in Yup'ik, it can refer to any sock, not necessarily one that belongs to a particular pair. Again, the Norton Sound Eskimos and apparently the Alaska Indians came up with a shortcut term for "other one of a pair," calling it "one-side"—or, as the Indian children said it, "other-side"—sock, shoe, glove, mitten.

When I entered a boarding school for Alaska Natives from across the state, I began to hear "I joke" or "I jokes" or "I kid," usually said with a smirk after making a remark in jest. The one that came closest to what we say in Yup'ik was "I lie," which my Athabascan Indian friends from Allakaket used. If I told a fib in jest to a fellow Yup'ik speaker, I said, "*Iqluamken*" (I am lying to you). Since Yup'ik has no word for "joke" or "kid," the listener infers the seriousness of "the lie" from context and from the speaker's body language.

For example, my cousin, then a mischievous teenager, said he played an April fool's trick on my unsuspecting grandfather, whom we called *Aataq* or *Aat* (meaning, "father"). Back when the Bethel-area schoolteachers represented various agencies in Bethel, my cousin told Grandpa that the teacher wanted to see him. Mumbling to himself, Grandpa started walking to the school. When he was almost there, my cousin hollered, "*Aat, iqluamken*" (Aat, I'm lying to you), laughing as he delivered the message. Incidentally, Grandpa knew nothing about April Fool's Day.

Recently, when I told a local schoolteacher, who had just moved to Alaska from Oklahoma, about the subject of this writing, he wondered about the local meaning of the word, "always," as in "Do you always play basketball?" (Actually, the children probably asked, "You always play basketball?") The schoolteacher jokingly answered the question, "No, sometimes I eat and sleep" because the teacher interpreted the word "always" as "all the time" or "continuously," as the *Random House Webster's College Dictionary* defines it, instead of understanding it the way his Norton Sound students and many rural Alaska residents use it.

According to the *Yup'ik Eskimo Dictionary*, both the Norton Sound and Kuskokwim Yup'ik speakers use the suffix *lar*, which means "to [verb] customarily; to [verb] regularly." Thus, the students were asking their teacher if he played basketball regularly—for instance, every Monday and Wednesday. Whenever I run across this suffix in a Yup'ik word and need to translate it into English, I'm never quite happy using "usually," which is the word I...ah...usually use.

To my way of thinking, it's hard not to think of "regularly" as "always." The opposite of "always," of course, is "never," also with a special usage in rural Alaska. Until I visited my folks' village, Nunapitchuk, in October 1999, I thought only village English speakers used the word "never" in this special way. At that time, my sister Sophia, who had learned "school English" as I had, asked her ten-year-old daughter in English, "Did you break your sister's toy?" To my surprise, my niece replied, "No, I never," instead of "No, I didn't," as her mother would have answered. In a personal communication with Steven Jacobson, I recounted the incident and wondered how the nonstandard usage of the word "never" could have entered my niece's English. He didn't know, but he did say that the word "never" levels the two verb forms in standard English, which are didn't or doesn't' and haven't or hasn't. My niece had adopted the statement, "I never," in place of the standard, "I didn't."

Instead of trying to figure out the correct way to form English verbs, the Norton Sound English speakers simply collapse it all to the word "never"—as in "I never eat" or "He, she or it never eat yet." It's much simpler that way, I admit, especially since Yup'ik uses only two suffixes to mark the past tense.

One summer, I attended a church service in Elim where a three-year-old girl and her mother were sitting nearby. As the worshipers filed out of the church at the end of the service, I saw the mother helping the little girl with her shoes, saying not too happily, "Even I tell you." Apparently, the mother had told her daughter to put on her shoes as the church service came to a close, but the little girl hadn't complied.

According to Jacobson, "In Yup'ik-influenced English, the conjunctions 'even if' and 'even though' are replaced by the single word 'even.'" Someone may say of a man in the village, "He always share his catch even he's real poor." Translated into standard English, the person is saying something akin to, "He shares his catch even though he's really poor." One time, too, an older sister ordered a twelve-year-old sibling to dump the dirty laundry water into the kitchen sink. "But the sink is too small," the younger girl protested. "Even," the older sister replied. This is probably another example of leveling, where the word "even" replaces the longer statement, "It doesn't matter." The process of trying to figure out the differences between the conjunctions, "even though" and "even if" gets a bit complicated, I think, so why not just say "even"?

When I was growing up, one of the first English words I heard from Yup'ik speakers was the word "bum." A toddler who refused to share a toy may be told, "Bum!" to let him or her know that his or her behavior was unacceptable. This easy-to-pronounce word probably replaced "bad" or "no good," for which we have a word but which sounds too severe in Yup'ik. I remember that the word was mastered easily by toddlers who wished to make known their opinion about another child or that child's behavior.

One of the first English words I heard growing up was "bum." A toddler who refused to share a toy may be told, "Bum!" to let him know his behavior was unacceptable.

Those of us who grew up speaking Yup'ik often laugh about the way we used to speak English. If an English sound we needed was missing from the Yup'ik language sound system, we simply used a Yup'ik sound that came closest to the English sound. For instance, since Yup'ik lacks the English "o," as in "boat," we would use the "u" sound, as in "parachute," and just say "boot," when we mean to say, "boat."

Perhaps the hardest English sound for a Yup'ik speaker to master is the troublesome "sh" sound. Since the Yup'ik language lacks that sound, "shallow" becomes "sallow" and "mission" sounds like it's "missin'." Once a good friend had to delay washing (or was it "wassing") her hair because the dormitory parent at her boarding school simply could not decipher "sampoo."

Consider the ways American English speakers play tricks on us. After laboriously learning to pronounce the "t" in "water" as the "t" in "toy," we notice that English speakers pronounce it more like a "d." One of the most "bugging" (a good Norton Sound expression) tricks yet is to learn to pronounce the middle "t" in "dentist" as the honest-to-goodness English "t" but to hear an English speaker pronounce it "dennist."

Now, the phrase "going to" is not an easy string of sounds for a Yup'ik speaker to master. When my Yup'ik-speaking friend was babysitting two English-speaking boys, she told one who was climbing around, "You are going to fall down." Before then, I had used "gonna" and had thought it sounded "cool." In high school, however, my freshman English teacher informed me that "gonna" was an improper usage, that "going to" was proper.

In school, we faithfully learned the plural forms of English nouns simply by attaching "s" or "es." Then one day a friend asked, "Where's the ack?" Well, since "ax" ends in an "s" sound, "ack" must be the singular of "ax." Much later when I was a student at UA Fairbanks, a group of Copper River Indians performed dances on campus. One of the songs they sang was, "Oh, We Go Fairbank." That there simply cannot be more than one makes perfect sense to me.

Once I overheard two high-school boys discussing in Yup'ik the status of a couple of their friends who had a boyfriend-girlfriend relationship. When one boy asked about the two, the other answered, "*Navgutellruuk*," (meaning, "The two broke each other"). Using a Yup'ik word *navg*, meaning, "to break," as only glass or a motor or toy might, the youth coined a nonstandard Yup'ik word to say, "The two of them broke up," for which no Yup'ik term exists to describe such a situation. Since we adopted the idea of a steady boyfriend-girlfriend relationship from the western culture, there's no Yup'ik word to describe the end of such a relationship. In our culture, only a married couple separates, and we haven't had to account for the break-up of a boyfriend and girlfriend until about the 1960s, perhaps. Did the boys, therefore, create Yup'ik slang?

In addition to coining words or phrases to describe situations that were nonexistent before our introduction to the Western culture, the Yup'ik Eskimos have borrowed words for objects or occupational positions from Russian and English. For instance, because flour, sugar, coffee, and tea apparently were brought to the Yup'ik Eskimos by the Russians, the words we use for these items are "Yup'ikized" Russian words. Flour is *mukaaq*; sugar is *saarralaq*, coffee *kuuvviaq*, and tea *saayuq*. When I was growing up, a pair of shoes was a novelty, but I called my pair *slip'essaak*. I admit my "pair of shoes" bore no resemblance to the English word "shoes," but my word *slip'essaak* comes from the English word for "slippers."

The most ingenious borrowed word to me is *espaak* (spark plug). Lacking the English "r" sound and unable to form a double consonant, such as "sp" at the beginning or end of a Yup'ik word, the Yup'ik speakers added a vowel at the beginning of the word "spark," dropped the foreign-sounding "r," and ignored "plug" altogether to coin the word *espaak* to mean "spark plug."

In other cases, the Yup'ik Eskimos simply created new words when introduced to new things. Take, for example, the word for a pair of pliers. What does a pair of pliers do? They "bite," right? Hence, I presume that the word *keggsuutek* ("two devices for biting)" comes from the two handles and "teeth" of the pliers. Then when the airplane came along, the Yup'ik Eskimos created the word *tengssuun* ("a device for flying") to describe the flying object and *tengssuuciurta* ("one who handles the 'device for flying'") to describe the pilot.

When a Yup'ik speaker learns to speak English, he or she thinks in Yup'ik and attempts to translate what he or she is thinking into English. This can be an arduous job. To search for English words that adequately portray the subtleties of the Yup'ik language is even harder. The Norton Sound Eskimos have done an admirable job of getting a handle on some of these subtle shades of meaning, often creating their own unique brand of English in the process.

As a Yup'ik speaker learning to speak English, I've encountered ridicule for my inability to produce the correct sounds. This, I admit, hasn't been fun. However, I would not trade my ability to operate in two languages, because I gain a deeper appreciation for both languages—Yup'ik, which didn't take any effort to learn, and English, which I'm still learning.

LUCY NUQARRLUK DANIELS, born in 1946, lived in Golovin, Alaska, for almost thirteen years. A Central Yup'ik, she has raised two children. Born into a family of nine children, she grew up in the lower Kuskokwim area of southwest Alaska. Her family lived a subsistence lifestyle. "Our primary food was fish, which we dried and smoked in the summer and put away for the winter," she recalls. "Today, we still depend on fish and moose for sustenance, though not to the extent we did when I was a child." Lucy earned a bachelor's degree in Yup'ik Eskimo at the University of Alaska Fairbanks and completed a secondary teaching certificate with an endorsement in history. She is currently working toward a master's degree in education. In addition, she has received training to assist victims of abuse. She and her family live in Soldotna, Alaska, on the Kenai Peninsula.

Deering, 1925

31

* * * * * * * * * * * *

~ DEERING ~

Television changes arctic rhythms
Al Bowling

I WAS FIVE WHEN I SAW MY FIRST television set, but by the mid-1950s, like most of the homes in the Lower 48, our family's television sat permanently anchored to its living room mooring.

I'd gawk nightly at rosters of electronic imagery that included *Have Gun Will Travel*, *I Love Lucy*, *The Twilight Zone*, *Rawhide*, *Mr. Ed*, *MASH*, *I Dream of Jeannie*, *The Beverly Hillbillies*, *Hogan's Heroes*, *Star Trek*, *The Fugitive*, *Bonanza*, and *Gilligan's Island* as well as professional sports on the weekends. Like a tomcat licking cream from a bowl, I lapped up every TV drop well into adulthood.

In August 1978, a twin-engine Islander touching down on the gravel airstrip in tiny Deering dropped my wife and me into a place near the Arctic Circle where commercial TV remained an alien creature, and I soon realized the wisdom in seeking alternative forms of recreation.

"Visiting" ranked high on the slate of entertainment options in this coastal Iñupiaq Eskimo village in northwest Alaska. My wife and I must have presented ourselves as curious creatures for observation in our home.

Indeed, if we didn't make the local kids leave, our constant stream of visitors probably would have camped overnight. Adults occasionally dropped in unannounced, too, and we'd boil water to chat over tea. Several people became regulars for cribbage.

For a change of scenery, we made unannounced calls ourselves, winding up at a neighbor's kitchen table drinking mugs of coffee and gobbling down cookies. Jigsaw puzzles in various stages of assembly inhabited tabletops throughout the village. In those pre-television days of rural Alaska, the variety of available recreational activities was directly linked to an individual's resourcefulness and ingenuity.

In local homes, bookcases laden with recycled paperbacks lined the walls, and someone always seemed to be curled up on a couch reading. I often saw folks lugging armfuls of books heading somewhere to exchange reading material. The really exciting books jumped from home to home like a common cold.

In those pre-television days, the variety of available recreational activities in the village was directly linked to an individual's resourcefulness and ingenuity.

In addition to their reading habit, local people listened to a nightly National Public Radio program titled *The Reader*, broadcast over the region's lone radio station, KOTZ, from Kotzebue. During Dick Estelle's thirty-minute monopoly on my time each evening, I strained to hear every word while ignoring tiny hands rapping at my door. Gradually, thoughts of my earlier TV habits became less frequent as I withdrew cold turkey.

On the east end of the village stood Deering's community building, which hosted recreational events, including bingo and movies. The city regularly rented sixteen-millimeter films from Anchorage. Every Friday night after school, someone from the school ran shows, and selected students worked popcorn duty. By six-thirty when the first viewers began arriving, we had the popcorn bagged, the projector loaded, the screen erected, and the folding chairs unfolded and aligned to seat anywhere from half to three-quarters of the entire village. As a result, almost everyone who lived in Deering saw each other at least once a week.

On the day following Christmas, local Eskimo games commenced. These mini-Olympics catapulted to the forefront of everyone's conversation, as virtually every community member joined one of two teams.

When a game began, each side sent out its smallest warrior. If a participant won, he or she remained on the floor, while the loser sat down. The losing team then would send out its next largest competitor. The contest continued until all the members of one team lost. The winning team was awarded one point, and the score was recorded on an official tally sheet as each game concluded.

For five evenings we jostled, taunted, hopped, tugged, pushed, laughed, and arm-wrestled. Surely we would have high-fived each other, too, but that gesture hadn't reached those parts yet. By this time of the year, television had faded completely from my mind.

In June 1979, I left Deering to digest more college courses before returning in January 1983 for three more years. During my absence, the Rural Alaska Television Network, or RATNet, began beaming commercial television via satellite to Deering and scores of other isolated communities throughout rural Alaska.

I didn't conduct any objective testing, but it seemed as if the insidious addiction nagging me when I first landed in Deering now had a firm grip on most of its residents. Reading for pleasure dropped off dramatically, with fewer people reading fewer books. Bookcases became lined with videotapes, and the Friday night movies disappeared. "Visiting" also dropped off dramatically.

Interest in *The Reader* also diminished, until the regional radio station stopped carrying that program. All of a sudden, it seemed, the National Football League had replaced traditional Eskimo games in Deering.

ALBERT BOWLING, born in 1946, lives in Anchorage with his wife, Jackie. He works as a billing clerk for Denali Anesthesia; in the past, he has been a teacher, pharmacy technician, and medical technologist. He describes himself as a "photography enthusiast." He lived in rural Alaska for many years, including Deering and Kotzebue. He holds a bachelor of science degree in medical technology from the University of Montana. The best thing about rural Alaska, he says, is "the simplicity of life."

The unusual stampede start of the annual Kobuk
440 Sled Dog Race on the sea ice along Front Street in
Kotzebue is a cherished tradition in northwest Alaska,
just like its endearing regional expression, "Adii."

32

. . . .

~ KOTZEBUE ~

"Adii": a common catch-all expression
Katie Cruthers

WEARILY, I WALK INTO OUR HOUSE and slowly lumber to the couch, where I plop down to rest for a few minutes. My husband strolls into the room and says, "Hi, honey. How was your day?"

"Adii, I am so tired," I say with a sigh. "It has been a long day."

Like most people from northwest Alaska, I frequently use the Iñupiaq word *adii*, which in modern times is pronounced "uh-dee." Consequently, someone, and usually people who have not lived in this region all their lives, eventually ask, "What does 'adii' mean?"

Adii is difficult to define because when we use this word, it involves the mood of the person and the situation. Each time the meaning varies depending on context. *Adii* may sharpen a negative response in one instance yet may soften the blow of being rejected in another.

"Adii" is difficult to define because when we use this word, it involves the mood of the person and the situation. Each time the meaning varies depending on context.

The expression *adii* originated from the Iñupiaq word *arii*, which means "ouch," Ruth Tatqavin Sampson explained to me. Now deceased, Ruth worked for many years in bilingual education at the Northwest Arctic Borough School District in Kotzebue. She said that the "r" in *arii* gradually

was changed to "d" because the new English-speaking generation of regional Iñupiaq people had a difficult time pronouncing
the "r" in *arii*. The Iñupiaq "r" is pronounced with a hint of the
sound "z," and it is difficult to verbalize accurately that sound,
she said. In any case, there is a variety of ways that *adii* is used in
modern Iñupiaq society, depending on the circumstances. Here
are a few:

1. To emphasize what you are saying. When someone wants to
   communicate to a friend how exhausted he or she is, that person would say, "*Adii*, I am tired." Similarly, in western culture,
   that person would say, "Man, I am tired." In this example, *adii*
   has about the same usage as the word "man." However, in this
   context, *adii* also adds the sense of being especially exhausted
   and expresses the unhappiness a person feels about it.

2. To express the word "no." When someone asks a person if he
   or she would like to take a walk, and he or she simply answers,
   "*Adii*," that means no. This usage also conveys that just the
   thought of taking a walk makes the person want to groan. It
   subtly stresses that there is no way to change your mind, as if
   to say, "Absolutely not!" in a polite way.

3. To show pain. If someone dies and a person feels the emotional
   pain of the loss that person may holler "*Adii*" while crying. In
   this case, sometimes *arii* is still used instead. This instance
   expresses the overwhelming emotional and nearly physical
   pain that a person is going through. This usage helps to release
   the pain. Also, if someone gets a cut or a bruise, he or she may
   say *adii* or *arii* to express the physical pain instead of saying
   "ouch." How loud you say it often demonstrates the level of
   pain you feel.

4. To show anger, irritation, or exasperation. When someone is
   being bothered and annoyed, he or she says, "*Adii*, stop it!" This
   shows exasperation. When a child is getting on Mom's nerves
   and Mom says, "*Adii!*" loudly and with force, the child knows
   that she has reached her limit and should not push it.

5. To get attention. Instead of sighing, a person may say *"adii"* quietly to express boredom. The implied message is that the person would like something to do or wish that someone would give him or her something to do. This method similarly is used to get attention from a friend when people want to talk about something that is bothering them. If someone quietly says *adii*, a friend will pick up on it and ask what is wrong.

6. To show pride and surprise. When a child shows unexpected progress and Dad wants to share the news with others, he may say, *"Adii*, my son. Today he took five steps all by himself!" This example shows how surprised and proud a parent is in what the child has accomplished, but it is not viewed as bragging. In this case, it is a positive experience and is used in a positive context.

7. To show sympathy or empathy. When someone talks to a friend about trouble at work, say with a co-worker, the friend can show empathy by saying, *"Adii*, poor you," meaning he or she understands and shares the unhappiness with the co-worker.

8. To show frustration, dislike, or unhappiness. When someone is known to be rude and obnoxious, for instance, cutting in front of everyone in the grocery store line, you may say to your friend, *"Adii*, so mean and rude!" If the focus is on an inanimate object, one might say, *"Adii*, this DVD player is impossible to figure out!" These examples illustrate variations in the feelings of frustration, dislike, or unhappiness.

9. To express being startled. When a person is startled or shocked, he or she may react by saying, *"Adii!"* Comparatively, one would just scream out loud or say "Oh, my god."

Although *adii* is considered an Iñupiaq word exclusive to northwest Alaska, many who move to this region pick it up because it is used so often. So many people come to Kotzebue and the surrounding villages for temporary positions at, say, the hospital or schools, that it would not be unreasonable to think that this catch-all might one day be heard throughout America and appear in the English dictionaries with multiple meanings.

KATIE QALINGAK CRUTHERS was born in 1970 and raised in Selawik, Alaska by her grandparents, Ray and Esther Skin. She was brought up in a traditional Iñupiaq lifestyle. A Selawik High School graduate, she continued her studies at the University of Alaska Fairbanks and Chukchi Campus in Kotzebue. She credits her mom, Alice Mitchell; her mother-in-law, Helga Larson, and her aunt, Ruthie Tatqavin Sampson, for supporting her efforts to learn and succeed. Katie has been married to Mark Cruthers since 1990. They have two sons. She has worked as grants administrator for the Southcentral Foundation; executive director for the Boys & Girls Clubs of northwest Alaska; administrator for Alaska Technical Center, and program-development specialist for the University of Alaska's Chukchi Campus. She lives in southcentral Alaska where she works for the Knik Tribal Council and teaches Iñupiaq through distance education.

Historic photo of Iñupiaq hunter watching
for seal near Nome, circa 1896-1913

INDEX

✳

Drifts bury the co-editors' Kotzebue home up to the rooflines
after a series of blizzards in February and March, 2009.

ABOUT THE CO-EDITORS

Professors John Creed and Susan Andrews with their children in
August 2006: front—twins Deirdre and Trevor, back—Tiffany and Myles

SUSAN B. ANDREWS lives north of the Arctic Circle in
Kotzebue, Alaska, with her husband, John Creed, and family.
Susan is professor of journalism and humanities at the Kotzebue
branch of the University of Alaska, Chukchi College, where she
has taught since 1989. Her students attend class via computer-assisted distance education primarily from remote villages
throughout rural Alaska. Prior to joining the UA faculty, Susan
was a television producer for the Kotzebue-based Northwest
Arctic Borough School District, creating television documentaries
on Alaska Native issues. Before coming to Kotzebue, she was anchor and news director at KTVF-TV, the CBS affiliate in Fairbanks.

A former ballet dancer, Susan completed her graduate work
in journalism at the University of Oregon following a compara-
tive-literature degree from Smith College in Massachusetts. As an
undergraduate she also attended the University of Paris.

Professor Andrews is the co-editor with John Creed of the
anthology, *Authentic Alaska: Voices of Its Native Writers*, recipient
of a Certificate of Commendation from the American Association
for State and Local History. Susan's writing interests include fic-
tion, non-fiction, and poetry. She loves living in Kotzebue for
"being able to walk everywhere and having the time with family

that otherwise would be spent commuting and running errands." Pastimes include yoga, reading, and cooking.

JOHN CREED is also professor of journalism and humanities at the University of Alaska's Chukchi College in Kotzebue, where he has distance taught students throughout Alaska since 1987. Before joining the UA faculty, he covered business and education for the *Fairbanks Daily News-Miner*. He also edited the *Tusraayugaat*, a bilingual newspaper published in the early 1980s by the Kotzebue-based Northwest Arctic School District. He also has taught school in Sutton, Massachusetts, and in Noatak, an Iñupiaq village north of Kotzebue.

Professor Creed studied English at the University of Massachusetts, Irish literature and history at University College Dublin in Ireland, physical education at the University of Oslo in Norway, and teacher education at the University of Montana. He completed his graduate work in journalism at the University of Oregon. He enjoys skiing, mountain biking, reading, and writing. The best thing about living in rural Alaska, he says, is "being able to raise a close-knit family at a much slower pace than mainstream American life."

In the late 1980s John and Susan founded Chukchi News and Information Service, a cultural journalism project that features University of Alaska student writing in newspapers, magazines, anthologies, and on websites. The anthology *Authentic Alaska: Voices of Its Native Writers* was compiled from the Chukchi News and Information Service project, winner of a Robert F. Kennedy Journalism Award and the Alaska Press Club's Public Service Award. They also have received awards for their work from the American Bar Association, Alaska Civil Liberties Union, and the American Lung Association of Alaska.

John and Susan have four children: Myles, born in 1989; Tiffany, born in 1990; and twins Trevor and Deirdre, born in 1996. The Creed children all have attended public schools in Kotzebue. Myles and Tiffany both graduated from Mt. Edgecumbe High School in Sitka, a public boarding school in southeast Alaska, before attending college in Portland, Oregon.

PHOTO CREDITS

SPECIAL THANKS to the following Alaska photographers for their contributions to this anthology: Al Bowling, Kotzebue/Anchorage; Nick Jans, Ambler/Juneau; James Magdanz, Kotzebue; Robert A. Andrews, Hollis; Seth Kantner, Kotzebue; R.A. Dillon, Kotzebue/Washington, D.C.; and Duane Nelson of Nelson's Photography, Fairbanks.

Title Page: Al Bowling

Table of Contents

Page 9: University of Alaska Museum of the North, Charlie Ott Collection, accession number UAP1983-046-001

Introduction

Page 12: John Creed

Survival

Page 18: Al Bowling

Page 22: Nellie Woods in traditional parka, John Creed

Page 22: Close-up of Nellie Woods, Steve Werle

Page 29: Alaska State Library, Dr. Daniel S. Neuman Collection, accession number ASL-P307-0078

Page 35: John Creed

Page 37: James Magdanz

Page 38: John Creed

Page 45: Nelson's Photography, Fairbanks, Alaska

Pages 46 & 51: courtesy John and Iva Baker

Pages 52 & 57: courtesy R. A. Dillon

Pages 58 & 62: courtesy Nancy Berkey

Page 64: Robert A. Andrews

Page 68: courtesy Marcus Miller

Page 70: John Creed.

Page 75: courtesy Karl Puckett

Page 76: courtesy Burton W. Haviland Jr.

Page 106: Al Bowling

Growing Up in Rural Alaska

Page 108: Anchorage Museum of History and Art Archives, accession number B62.x.22.6

Page 110: Anchorage Museum of History and Art Archives, accession number B75.134.54

Pages 112 & 115: John Creed

Pages 116 & 121: courtesy Gina Pope

Page 122: John Creed

Page 128: Al Bowling

Page 130: Nick Jans

Page 135: Caroline Sanders

Pages 136 & 140: courtesy Sonja Whitethorn

Page 142: John Creed

Page 150: Jerry Daniels

Pages 152 & 156: Seth Kantner

Harvesting the Land and Sea

Page 158: Alaska State Library, Harry T. Becker Collection, accession number ASL-P67-176

Page 162: Alaska State Library, Skinner Foundation Collection, accession number ASL-P44-01-07

Page 167: courtesy Sonja Whitethorn

Pages 168 & 177: Nick Jans

Page 178: Seth Kantner

Page 182: courtesy Emma Snyder

Generations

Page 184: Anchorage Museum of History and Art Archives, accession number B70.60.5.

Page 188: courtesy John Creed

Page 193: Will Boger

Page 194: Al Bowling

Pages 197, 199 & 205: John Creed

Pages 206 & 210: John Creed

Page 215: Nelson's Photography, Fairbanks, Alaska

Pages 216 & 220: James Magdanz

Page 221: Nelson's Photography, Fairbanks, Alaska

Pages 222 & 227: courtesy Sonja Whitethorn

Recreation

Page 228: R.A. Dillon

Pages 232 & 240: courtesy Robert A. Andrews

Page 242: Al Bowling

Page 246: courtesy Iva Baker

Pages 248 &253: courtesy Kathy Lenniger

Culture

Page 254: courtesy Alaska State Library, William R. Norton Collection, accession number ASL-P226-195

Pages 258 & 260: Al Bowling

Page 261: courtesy Wilma C. Payne

Page 262: Al Bowling

Page 265: courtesy Gina Pope

Pages 266 & 271: courtesy Terry Wilson

Page 272: Nick Jans

Page 281: Jerry Daniels

Portrait of a pike, Pah River

Recommendations for readers seeking a greater understanding of Alaska's rural people

BIRD GIRL & THE MAN WHO FOLLOWED THE SUN
An Athabascan Indian Legend from Alaska
Velma Wallis, hardbound, $19.95

COLD RIVER SPIRITS
The Legacy of an Athabascan-Irish Family from Alaska
Jan Harper-Haines, hardbound, $19.95

MOMENTS RIGHTLY PLACED
An Aleutian Memoir
Ray Hudson, trade paperback, $14.95

RAISING OURSELVES
A Gwitch'in Coming of Age Story from the Yukon River
Velma Wallis, trade paperback, $15.95

SEVEN WORDS FOR WIND
Essays and Field Notes from Alaska's Pribilof Islands
Sumner MacLeish, hardbound, $16.95

SPIRIT OF THE WIND
*The Story of Alaska's George Attla,
Legendary Sled Dog Sprint Champ*
Lew Freedman, trade paperback, $14.95

SURVIVING THE ISLAND OF GRACE
A Life on the Wild Edge of America
Leslie Leyland Fields, trade paperback, $17.95

TWO OLD WOMEN
An Alaska Legend of Betrayal, Courage, and Survival
Velma Wallis, hardbound, $16.95

Epicenter Press
Alaska Book Adventures™

These titles can be found or special-ordered at your local bookstore. A wide assortment of other Alaska books also can be ordered from the publisher's website, www.EpicenterPress.com, or by calling 1-800-950-6663.